PETER ADEGBIE

MAXIMIZING BUSINESS ADVANTAGE

THE JOSHUA REVELATION

MAXIMIZING BUSINESS SUCCESS

THE JOSHUA REVELATION

BY
PETER ADEGBIE

Copyright 2015

Peter Kayode Adegbie

ISBN 978-1-911109-01-3

Published in the United Kingdom by GOLDEN POT MEDIA.

Cover Design and Page Layout
Kenteba Kreations
www.kentebakreations.com

All rights reserved. No portion of this book may be used without the written permission of the publisher, with the exception of brief excerpts in magazines, articles, reviews etc.
For further information or permission, address:
Golden Pot Media
MICC Cornhill Road
SR5 1RU
Website:Goldenpotmedia.com
E-mail:pastorpeter@goldenpot.com
:adegbiepk@yahoo.com

All scripture quotations are from the King James Version of the Bible except otherwise stated.

DEDICATION

This book is dedicated to my parents, two blessed and precious people who made a success of the business of life, late Mr. Henry Adegbie and Mrs. Mary Adegbie.

APPRECIATION

I deeply appreciate the Lord God, the Almighty father for giving me the unique privilege of writing this book.

I appreciate the mentors in my life, Bishop and Pastor Mrs Wesley Arije, Apostle Dr. and Pastor Mrs John Ameobi, Pastor Clem and Majorie Esomowei and Dr. Raymond Dennis. It is a great privilege for me to serve. I want to deeply appreciate my wife Theodora Nkechi Oluwafunmilayo for her love and companionship, sweetheart you are God's gift to me thank you. I remain eternally indebted to the grace and lovingkindness of the most precious Holy Spirit. Thanks a million sweet and glorious one for revealing yourself and glorifying Jesus.

CONTENTS

DEDICATION	3
APPRECIATION	4
FIRST WORDS	6
INTRODUCTION	9
LAW OF APPROPRIATION	17
THE LAW OF VISION	31
THE LAW OF PREPARATION	39
THE LAW OF OBEDIENCE	49
THE LAW OF RECOGNITION	71
THE LAW OF IDENTIFICATION	89

FIRST WORDS

...This book was divinely inspired...

25th August 2000, Douala Cameroon…

"This is a book about success, it's loaded with business principles and every business man and woman ought to read it."

I was in my study, as resident pastor of the Living Faith Church in Douala, Cameroon, preparing for the monthly Breakthrough Seminar. I characteristically seek God's face frantically before any of the seminars I was privileged to conduct, but this time it was different. I tried to pray, and it was like heaven had turned to brass; I sang praises and worshipped yet there was restlessness in my spirit I could not understand so I decided to fast but to no avail. What I felt in my spirit was a burden I could not explain.

When I finally gave up trying to figure out what was happening to me, I picked up my Bible and flopped on the bed. I casually flipped open to the book of Joshua and then the Lord said, "This is a book about success, it's loaded with business principles every business man and woman ought to read". I was startled, but then the Lord opened my eyes and right from the first verse in the first chapter He began to reveal certain principles to me and

I ended up sharing some of the principles at the seminar. That is the origin of this book. It is by no means exhaustive however it examines the book of Joshua and reveals certain unique principles on the conquest of Canaan, because our future success is like a Canaan that God expects us to conquer.

I believe that the Lord who inspired the revelation will inspire your heart and quicken your understanding to maximize the impact of the business of your life in Jesus name.

In my attempt to research and flesh out the points revealed to me in this work, I have included some writings and quotations of great Christian men and women whom I have tried to acknowledge, except for a few omissions where the authors are unknown.

You shall succeed.

KING OF FAVOUR AND FORTUNE

The shadow of His countenance
But the brightness of midday sun
In His smile, daylight is but a joke
He that fails not
In His word is His bond
Everlasting and sure His trail
In awesomeness, intimidating
In love comforting
In mercy rich and kind
Wonderful Lord
In you my reward is sure
Prosperity and abundance my
Foundation stones
Goodness and mercy my companions
I rejoice and abound into eternity
In your words and promises
A hundred fold due me?
What generosity, what magnanimity
My heart is set to dine in the fatness of your courts
My soul rejoices in the revelation of your wisdom
Like Daniel make me ten times better
For the King of fortune has favoured me
I am crowned with glory and honour
I walk majestically as his jewel
In His courts to dwell forever more

Peter Kayode Adegbie

INTRODUCTION

Why the book of Joshua for business success?

There are five reasons we can readily identify:

1. It is a book about success

> "This book of the law shall not depart out of thy mouth, but thou shalt meditate therein day and night, that thou mayest observe to do according to all that is written therein; for then thou shalt make thy way prosperous, and then thou shalt have good success"
> Joshua 1:8.

In this book, our focus is on how to enjoy good success, and only God sets the true standard of success. "His blessings makes rich and adds no sorrow", Proverbs 10:22. When you follow the standard of success He came to establish for us, He will bless you in peaceful, pleasant and favourable ways beyond your imagination.

2. It is a book about faith and courage

> "Only be thou strong and very courageous…"
> "…Be strong and of a good courage…"
> Joshua 1: 7,9.

Faith and courage are strong currents in the book of Joshua. These qualities are necessary ingredients for success in any business, especially the business of life. Whatever you do, you need to put your trust absolutely in God. Courage is a product of trust in the Lord, only when you are strong in the word and promises of God can you be confident that He will display His power and might towards you.

> *"...Trust in the Lord with all thine heart; and lean not unto thine own understanding. In all thy ways acknowledge him, and he shall direct thy paths"*
> *Proverbs 3:5-6.*

It is only by trusting in Him and facing life courageously that we can please Him, when we please Him; He imparts the wisdom and courage we need to overcome the challenges of life.

3. It is a book on divine guidance

> *"And the Lord said unto Joshua, See, I have given into thine hand Jericho, and it's king thereof, and the mighty men of valour. And ye shall compass the city, all ye men of war, and go round about the city once. Thus shalt thou do six days ... and it shall come to pass, that when they make a long blast with the ram's horn, and when ye hear the sound of the trumpet, all the people shall shout with a great shout; and the wall of the city shall fall down flat, and the people shall ascend up, every man straight before him. "*
> *Joshua 6:2-5.*

There may not be genuine breakthrough in the business of life unless we receive God's guidance.

> *"Thus saith the Lord thy redeemer, the Holy one of Israel; I am the Lord thy God, which teacheth thee to profit, which leadeth thee by the way that thou shouldest go"*
> *Isaiah 48:17.*

INTRODUCTION

4. It's a book that profiles good leadership

> "...but as for me and my house, we will serve the Lord." "And Israel served the Lord all the days of Joshua..."
> Joshua 24:15,31.

God desires for you to be a leader. Didn't He say you should be above only and not beneath? Leadership begins with you making qualitative decisions. Leadership is commitment to personal integrity and truth. Leadership is also skillful human management.

> "So he fed them according to the integrity of his heart, and guided them by the skillfulness of his hands"
> Psalm 78:72.

5. It's a book about conquest

> "So Joshua took the whole land, according to all that the Lord said unto Moses; and Joshua gave it for an inheritance unto Israel according to their divisions by their tribes. And the land rested from war."
> Joshua 11:23

Church attendance and church activity do not satisfy God. He has provided a land flowing with milk and honey; He will never be satisfied with our singing and dancing in the wilderness. I don't think God is satisfied until we conquer our Canaan and enter into His rest. These are the five principles that underlie the teaching in this book.

Who is a businessman or woman?

A person who is engaged on a mission, venture, occupation, trade or pursuit with intent to make profit is in business. Locating the assignment may be the greatest challenge but pursuing it, with a desire to create advantage or benefit for yourself and others, is what makes you a businessman or woman.

Business is a process of investing to make profit. Everyone in business invests something with an expectation of some profit. There is always first a seed and then the harvest from the seed. If you are an investor who does not expect profit, you are not in business and you are ungodly because even God our heavenly father is profit oriented.

In Luke 19:13 the bible portrays God as an entrepreneur who expects profit from his investments
. "…And he called his ten servants, and delivered them ten pounds, and said unto them, Occupy till I come"

What does it mean to "occupy"? In this context, it means invest, get busy, profit from, expand, dominate, conquer, take over, invade, and take possession of.

God is interested in what you invest and how you invest because He desires that your investment should yield profit.

Dear friend, are you investing and occupying with your life?

> *"And it came to pass, that when he was returned having received the kingdom, then he commanded these servants to be called unto him, to whom he had given the money, that he might know how much every man had gained by trading"*
> *Luke 19:15*

INTRODUCTION

God asked them for an account of their investments because He was interested in their productivity and gain. If you are not making adequate progress and recording gain in your endeavors, perhaps you are working outside of God's methods. He expected them to gain by trading.

Whatever has been stagnant in your life has potential for divine motion because there is God's investment in you that He expects you to profit by.

God does not make unreasonable demands, He had given to every man according to their several abilities and He had a projection of what he expected as returns from each one of us.

His ways are superior, they cannot be hindered and no man can shut the door against his methods. (Isaiah 55:8-11, Revelations 3: 7)).

No one is on earth to just occupy space; this passage equates occupying to trading. In Luke 19:16-19, God was happy with those who traded and gained with what He gave them and He expressed his satisfaction by rewarding them. However there was one man whom God thought was worth at least one pound who proved himself to be worthless.

God was angry that he neither traded with nor allowed the latent power of the pound to bring gain so the pound was collected from him and interestingly; it was given to the man who had the best ability to maximize what was given to him.
The investment of God in your life will not be withdrawn in Jesus name. I pray that the Lord will bring great gain your way, as you are provoked to walk in his ways.

God as a businessman

God is very particular about profit and loss and every business success can be traced back to secrets discovered in His word. Every business explosion in righteousness can be ascribed to the author and perfecter of all things, our Father and our God. Only in His light can we become illuminated, He is the eternal fountain where we drink life's essence. He is the divine instructor who uncovers depths untold to bring profit into our lives. There are secrets concealed that God has not yet unveiled to us, but His words that He has revealed, are for us and our children to obey forever (Deuteronomy29: 29).

When we discover His higher ways and obey His dictates, He rewards us. Proverbs 24:13-14 says, Eat thou honey because it is good; and the honeycomb, which is sweet to thy taste: so shall the knowledge of wisdom be unto thy soul: when thou hast found it, then there shall be a reward and thine expectation shall not be cut off.

Every appointment with failure is disappointed when you find His wisdom because the knowledge of this wisdom will put a permanent end to frustration in your life.

His methods are sweeter than honey and they establish every expectation of success, His ways are ways of pleasantness, and all His paths are peace.

Jesus recognized early the business perspective of life.
In Luke 2:49, He said, ... how is it that ye sought me? Wist ye not that I must be about my fathers business?
He perceived life as a business, a business owned by God to whom we are responsible as custodians and co-labourers. It is not just ours to do as we wish but we are stewards who must give account of the life entrusted into our care.

INTRODUCTION

In the book of Acts 6:3, the Apostles looked for honest men that they …may appoint over this business. They saw their assignment and purpose in life also as a business.

God appreciates men and women, who understand their relationship with Him in this dimension; God loves people who are focused in their pursuits, and people of passion and purpose turn Him on.

Abraham was not a pastor; he was a cattle trader, yet the Bible called him, the friend of God. You can be God's friend in the business of your life too, no matter what you are specifically called to do.

Through this book may the power of God help you bring profit to the business of life, may the eyes of your understanding be enlightened as you encounter divine wisdom that will transform you into a distinguished businessman and woman. God is interested in your investments. Everything you have is a seed that can be invested: time, money, friendship, talent and skill are all precious seeds.

THE MASTER'S HAND

The master's hand
Write the pages of my life
In my daily search for his depth
In the longings of my soul
He stirs by his rod and Spirit
The core of my passion
This quest, this thirst like a
Deep melodious symphony
Sometimes I feel the caress of
His hands by the spirit and my life unfolds
In the magnitude of his love my life is a poem
In the sweetness of his voice I am but a song
Write master Jesus, write the chapters of my life
In your unending book of eternity
Everyday with you an adventure
Into wisdom and power
Write master Jesus write
Alpha and Omega writes in readiness
Into the glorious destiny of son-ship
Ordained for me
I see the words of my life and they are deep
I cannot comprehend
In the midst of my mystery
Your living Spirit springs the living water
In my soul to flow as the streams
From your throne
In the freshness of your breath
Is the richness and fertility of its banks
My mind now comprehends
What depth and beauty
What love and grace,
How profound your truth Lord
How wonderful your light
Write on Master Jesus
Write me on into eternity with you.

Peter Kayode Adegbie

CHAPTER ONE

LAW OF APPROPRIATION

"...Now therefore arise, go over this Jordan, thou and all this people, unto the land which I do give to them, even to the children of Israel. Every place that the sole of your feet shall tread upon, that have I given unto you, as I said unto Moses."
Joshua 1:2-3

"Blessed be the God and father of our Lord Jesus Christ, who hath blessed us with all spiritual blessings in heavenly places in Christ"
Ephesians 1:3.

This law says that certain things already belong to you, they are grants due to you, allotments you deserve, a divine subsidy from heaven, God's contribution that is in harmony with you. They are already provided for the business of your life; they are already allocated to you. All that is needed is for you to appropriate, and take them.

"Rise up, take your journey, and pass over the river Arnon: behold, I have given into thy hand Sihon the Amorite, king of Heshbon and his land, begin to possess it and contend with him in battle".
Deuteronomy 2:24

These divine provisions must be sought and contended for before you can possess or partake of them. However, many people hesitate beside River Arnon watching "Sihon" parade as king over a territory God has already given to them. I don't know what River Arnon is in your life, or what circumstances you have camped around and refused to get over; I do know that you need courage and determination to arise and step forward and take possession of what God has already allocated to you.

May the Holy Spirit ignite your heart to arise from where you have been camping in stagnation and take a step forward with God.

In Genesis 13:14-15,
"And the Lord said unto Abram, after that Lot was separated from Him, Lift up now thine eyes, and look from the place where thou art northward and southward, and eastward and westward. For all the land which thou seest to thee will I give it, and to thy seed forever".

You must part ways with the Lot of fear and procrastination, the Lot of self-doubt and inferiority complex, you need the courage to arise and step forward. You have camped around that place long enough; God has greater things in store for you. Many never look from the place where they are, so they waste their time and resources in mediocrity and never make progress. But wherever you are now, there are certain things God has already allocated for you to function and prosper in the business of your life. Why don't you step forward and take them.

A Japanese proverb says, "To wait for luck is the same as waiting for death." Similarly, Longfellow, in one of his poems said, "The divine insanity of noble minds, that never falters nor abates, but labours, and endures, and waits till all that it foresees it finds, or what it cannot find it creates."

God will open your eyes and you will step forward to take that which belongs to you when your desire is so strong that what you cannot find, you create. Then the struggles of your life shall be terminated and your frustration will come to an end. He said, "lift up now thine eyes"- your eyes of understanding and look from the place where you are, northwards, southwards, eastwards and westwards, for all the land that thou seest, to thee will I give it and to thy seed forever." Land is a type of life, what kind of life do you see ahead of you? The life and future you cannot see you cannot feature in. You must see beyond where you are to provoke the help of God. God told Joshua, "there is something you desire, it is time to arise and possess it, stop bemoaning Moses, he is gone, the past is irretrievable, only learn from the past; the future waits in anticipation of your courageous move."(Paraphrased).

Delay is not denial. God will never deny you what you are due. What delays your inheritance is fear; fear of the unknown, fear of the unfamiliar, fear to take a risk, fear that makes it convenient to hang around the foot of the most familiar mountain, making excuses. But God has been saying arise, there is something more for you; there is something greater inside you than what you are doing. May you discover that path of destiny; Anderson M. Baten said, "Weak men wait for opportunities: strong men make them."

The Lord dealt with Joshua as He did with Moses and I believe He still deals with us that same way. Moses said in Deuteronomy 1:6-8. "The Lord our God spake unto us in Horeb, saying, Ye have dwelt long enough in this mount: Turn you, and take your journey, and go to the mount of the Amorites, and unto all the places nigh thereunto, in the plain, in the hills, and in the vale, and in the south, and by the sea side, to the land of the Canaanites, and unto Lebanon, unto the great river, the river Euphrates"

He later testified of God's faithfulness in Deuteronomy 2:36. "From Aroer, which is by the brink of the river of Arnon and from the city that is by the river, even unto Gilead, there was not one city too strong for us: the Lord our God, delivered all unto us".

Now therefore arise, you must go over your own Jordan also, you are destined to cross over into Canaan. Every place that the sole of your feet shall tread upon, God is prepared to give you. But you must arise, and step forward. If you will make the commitment to step forward, God will fulfil His promise to give you the land. That victory and expectation is already given, go and take advantage of it.

Meditation: Step into the Waters
Hannah Whitall Smith

A man was obliged to descend into a deep well by sliding down a fixed rope, which was supposed to be of ample length. But to his dismay he came to the end of it before his feet had touched the bottom. He had not the strength to climb up again, and to let go and drop seemed to him but to be dashed to pieces in the depths below. He held on until his strength was utterly exhausted, and then dropped, as he thought to his death. He fell- just three inches - and found himself safe on the rock bottom.

Are you afraid to take this step? Does it seem too sudden, too much like a leap in the dark? Do you not know that the step of faith always "falls on the seeming void, but finds the rock beneath?" If ever you are to enter this glorious land, flowing with milk and honey, you must sooner or later step into the brimming waters, for there is no other path; and to do it now may save you months and even years of disappointment and grief. Hear the word of the Lord

-

"Have I not commanded thee? Be strong and of a good courage; be not afraid, neither be thou dismayed: for the Lord thy God is with thee, whithersoever thou goest"
Joshua 1:9

Three things enabled Joshua to step forward and fulfill his destiny.

The Bible says Joshua was Moses' minister.

"Now after the death of Moses the servant of the Lord, it came to pass, that the Lord spake unto Joshua the son of Nun, Moses' minister, saying..."
Joshua 1:1.

In Hebrew the word minister is "shârath", which means a menial attendant, or worshipper, a servant. In other words, he was Moses' servant in the business of managing God's people, an apprentice trained under Moses in the business of shepherding.

1. He stayed long enough under Moses to learn and understand the business. He was a committed and loyal servant under Moses.
2. He was trained in full submission under the commandment of Moses. He willingly and totally submitted himself to serve one man - Moses.
3. He was intimately associated with Moses. By that association, he became more than a servant, he knew what Moses would do in certain situations. He was able to work in the same spirit with Moses and this enabled him to continue the work on the business of Moses.

If you cannot complete your master's assignment, maybe you are not a good servant. Joshua was called into business as a servant and apprentice with the unique privilege of finishing the assignment his master began and he succeeded.

His call was not as spectacular as Moses; God simply said "Joshua, my servant Moses has prepared you, now I think you are mature enough to follow me, are you ready? When your earthly master completes his assignment of training you, you qualify to come under your eternal master. This was Joshua's call into business. The moment your master finishes his job of training you, you are ready to cross your Jordan. God defined the borders of Joshua, and defined his vision.

I don't know what vision you have for your life, and what will constitute your own challenge of faith? I can imagine Joshua at this point, with a master like Moses, a man who spoke with God face to face and single handedly performed all kinds of miracles.

A man whom God made a god unto Pharaoh, who with the rod of God parted the Red Sea, and made a mockery of the strength and wealth of Egypt, an extraordinary revolutionary whose feats are unequalled in the history of mankind. Yet God said to Joshua, arise, your training is enough, start the business of leadership now. It was a challenge of faith for Joshua, because the bible tells us that at that particular time, the river Jordan had just flooded its banks. There was flood. If you are a reasonable and responsible leader, flood time is not the best time to lead people across a river. But that was Joshua's challenge of faith, God seemingly said if you truly trust me, arise and cross the Jordan now. I don't know what your own challenge of faith is, but the truth is, in every business especially at the beginning, there are challenges of faith. However, if you have the confidence that it is God Almighty who defines your borders and establishes your purpose, you will march ahead with boldness and your greatest asset will be the ability and sensitivity to discern His voice and follow his leading.

In 1989 the Living Faith Church Worldwide under the leadership of David Oyedepo faced a unique challenge in Kaduna and in the midst of the apparent challenge, on the nineteenth of July God said to him, "Arise get down to Lagos and raise me a people". Today close to a fifty thousand strong congregation in the largest single church auditorium in the world attests to the supremacy of discerning and obeying God's voice.

Are you looking at the "flood" of the local economy or the "flood" of your meagre bank account or are you listening to God? Whatever constitutes that challenge of faith, when God says arise, you better do, because His presence is able to turn every obstacle into a miracle. Spurgeon said, "Many men owe the grandeur of their lives to their tremendous difficulties", and Phillips Brooks said, "Wherever souls are being tried and ripened, in whatever commonplace and homely way, there God is hewing out the pillars for His temple." Arise go over this Jordan! Is the Lord speaking to you right now? There is no business that doesn't have elements of risk. Have you been afraid to take that step of faith? I want your heart to receive courage now. What have you imagined for your business? What goals have you set your mind to achieve in life? There is much more potential in you than you know and until you invest your potential, God will not increase your ability neither would you improve your skill.

Look at the Bible and the history of God's dealing with man. Noah, Moses, Gideon, Paul, Peter, and the mother of our Lord, Mary, were all people who never believed God could use them, but God is a God who specialises in making somebody out of nobody. Whatever is your own challenge of faith, take courage, it is time to arise. The adventure and excitement is not at the foot of the mountain, the view is most beautiful at the top. Mountain climbing is however not for the faint hearted, the struggle to obtain knowledge and to advance one's self in the world will strengthen the mind, discipline the faculties, mature the senses, promote self-help, and give force of character.

The hand of God cannot be seen until you take steps of courage to cross that Jordan of fear and that hesitation in your heart, you will not fail but you will see the mighty hand of God. Let me share this testimony of my experience on the mission field.

When I arrived in the great nation of Cameroon on May 31, 1998, it was a Saturday, and after a brief drive with my missionary colleagues through the streets of Douala we got to the residence where my family was to live for the next year. The following morning was my first Sunday and the church service was held at the Labour union hall, which was used the previous night as a disco hall with free beer for whoever cares. The stench of liquor was still in the air that morning despite the efforts by the sanitation department of the church to deodorize the place.

Later that day we honoured an invitation to receive Dr. Margaret Idahosa at the ONCPB conference hall in Bonanjo, the largest and by far the most beautiful hall in the city. As I stepped into that building the Holy Spirit said to me "Why are you not worshipping here?" It was awesome, but very real. However looking at our circumstances at that time, it was absolutely ridiculous to expect our mission at the stage of its existence to afford a gorgeous place like that, nonetheless it was impossible to ignore the voice of the Holy Spirit.

When I began to make inquiries about the hall, everyone I talked to discouraged me because it was indeed too expensive. But I reckoned that if I heard God correctly I should give it my best shot. When I finally met the executives in charge, it was uncanny, because they received me as if they had been expecting me. In fact, one of them had read Bishop David Oyedepo's book on Releasing the Supernatural.

At the negotiation table, the Holy Spirit actually took over because I said things that I neither thought nor planned for. I discovered that the hall cost about 200,000cfa per day ($500). It was much too expensive for us especially when we had to pay in advance for six months. Right there while sitting, waiting to sign a contract for which I had no clue as to how to fulfil financially, the Holy Spirit came through to me so clearly in a word of wisdom. I suddenly found myself speaking boldly about the mission I was representing and I began to tell the authorities about our training and discipline, especially concerning time. I was able to convince them to rent the hall to us on an hourly basis and got the entire hall including two offices for 450,000cfa per month instead of 6,000,000 cfa at 200,000cfa per day.

I believe that because I stepped forward God imparted grace and courage to negotiate and get the place. There are things that are already allocated to you but you must arise with determination and appropriate them. Many have been sitting on the banks of Jordan staring at the tides of life as they ebb and flow. Why not conduct self-examination and you may discover that you already have what you need for that business to prosper. If you don't, then take appropriate steps to acquire the relevant skills, and apply them. It is time to step forward and take the risk associated with breakthrough. Winston Churchill said, "Kites rise highest against the wind, not with it." When you hesitate, is it because you are afraid? You test the water and because you can't feel anything familiar, you decide to quit or try again tomorrow. Take courage. Your blessing is across that Jordan. Don't sit on the fence. It is important to think, to plan, to organize and to pray. They have their own time and importance but there is also a time to act.

Two Kinds of Hesitation

When it is time to act, do you hesitate? It becomes important that you understand why you hesitate. There are two reasons, two kinds of hesitation:

1. When hesitation comes from your spirit man, it is a time to stop, research some more and pray before you go forward in that business, or make that investment of time, effort, finances and skill. The Holy Spirit may be warning you against something ahead that you are shortsighted about. Remember He searches all things even the deep things of God and knows the end from the beginning.
2. When hesitation is from your flesh, out of fear, because you are about to do something you have not done before, then brush it aside and step forward.

You must be able to discern prayerfully whether the hesitation is coming from your spirit or whether it is out of fleshly fear.

LAW OF APPROPRIATION

"...In nothing terrified by your adversaries, which is to them an evident token of perdition, but to you of salvation, and that of God"
Philippians 1:28

When you decide to march forward, you will discover God has been waiting for you all this while. If the Holy Spirit has led you, God will provide the resources and the wisdom you need. You don't have to fear you only need to step forward boldly and courageously. There are things He has prepared for you.

He is just waiting for you to trust Him. Until you demonstrate your trust in Him, and take practical steps, you may not see His manifestation. "They that trust in the Lord shall be like Mount Zion that cannot be moved but abideth forever. Psalms 125:1.

God has prepared something especially for you and you must appropriate it. God told Joshua that certain places are already given to him but he must appropriate them by physically stepping there with the soles of his feet. This connotes practical involvement.

"Every place the sole of your foot shall tread upon, that have I given unto you as I said unto Moses"
Joshua 1:3

You can never appropriate your inheritance until you are practically involved and you accept responsibility for your life. They crossed their Jordan by faith, they stepped into the flooded river with the ark of God. They took courage and they believed God's word as spoken to Joshua. From where you are, take a spiritual and prophetic step forward, and say "Lord every fear and every negative hesitation is over in my life today. I agree with you in my spirit and I step forward in my business." Step forward right now physically and prophesy into your life. "Lord every negative hesitation is over, I am stepping forward, and I am appropriating the things that belong to me." Get ready to be practically involved with the business of your life.

Our redemption in Christ is a comprehensive package on our journey into glory. When we are born again, we are not born again to suffer; we are born again to gain the abundance of heavenly treasures.

Psalms 103:1-5 reveals God's plan for us,

> *"Bless the Lord, O my soul: and all that is within me, bless his holy name. Bless the Lord, O my soul, and forget not his benefits: Who forgiveth all thine iniquities; who healeth all thy diseases; Who redeemeth thy life from destruction; who crowneth thee with lovingkindness and tender mercies; Who satisfieth thy mouth with good things; so that thy youth is renewed like the eagle's."*

This is a prophetic insight into God's heart for you. The bible tells us about the grace of our Lord Jesus Christ, that, though He was rich, yet because of us, He became poor that we through His poverty might become rich.

> *"For ye know the grace of our Lord Jesus Christ, that though he was rich, yet for your sakes he became poor, that ye through his poverty might be rich."*
> *2Corinthians 8:9*

This is not only referring to spiritual riches; it includes material and physical riches. God can take over your battles from today and show you favour in the business of your life. There is a purpose why God created you. Some lazy people have entered into the Church with the doctrine of "don't worry, God will do everything" so they do nothing because they are waiting for God, because they expect nothing they experience nothing. The Church is not a place for lazy people.

Nothing will make God happier than your success in the business of your life. As you are reading this book, the Spirit of God will quicken you, and set you up upon your feet for divine speed, in the direction God has allocated for you. You shall surely succeed. If you are in Christ, you are already blessed with all blessings in heavenly places (Ephesians 1:3), what is left is for you to step forward and appropriate those blessings.

> *"Pass through the host, and command the people, saying, Prepare you victuals; for within three days ye shall pass over this Jordan, to go in to possess the land, which the Lord your God giveth you to possess it."*
> *Joshua 1:11*

God told Joshua to pass through the host and command the people to prepare. He said that within three days they would pass over the River Jordan. I don't know what that Jordan is in your life, that has kept you down in one spot and your life has been going round in circles, but you can break that circle today in the name of Jesus Christ. Be determined to go forward; refuse to stand outside the door of your miracle. The miracle is across Jordan; be ready to cross. To go in, "…to possess the land, which the Lord giveth you to possess…" This word is for everyone who is called by God, every one who is born again. That is a prophetic word for you. Prepare and go in to possess what God had already prepared and gathered for you to possess.

> *"Behold I send an Angel before thee, to keep thee in the way, and to bring thee into the place which I have prepared"*
> *Exodus 23:20*

In this kingdom of God, there is an anointing to take all that God has prepared for you. Many people are born again but they never take all that belongs to them. Lazarus got to Heaven but he didn't take all that belonged to him here. Are you prepared for what God has prepared for you?

The Bible says Abraham was blessed in all things. There is an anointing to take all things and richly enjoy all things God has laid in store for you. In this kingdom, the enemy will try to contend with you for your inheritance, but you must take that which belongs to you by force.

> *"And from the days of John the Baptist until now the kingdom of heaven suffereth violence and the violent take it by force"*
> *Mathew 11:12*

The devil will try to discourage you, and advise you to wait till later but "Tomorrow will become the day after tomorrow." So says a Xhosa proverb from South Africa.

Joshua 11:16 "… so Joshua took." They did not give it to him, he took it, and you will have to take your own too. In verse 19, "There was not a city that made peace with the children of Israel save the Hivites the inhabitants of Gibeon: all other they took in battle" you must take your own too. In Verse 23 "… so Joshua took…" God has destined for you to get to the top. He has destined for your business to succeed. No enemy can stop your success. But you must be prepared to take. This leads us to the next law.

CHAPTER TWO

THE LAW OF VISION

"And the Lord said unto Joshua, See..."
Joshua 6:2

You can never take what you cannot see. May God open your eyes to see that which belongs to you. In 1John 1:1 "... that which was from the beginning which we have looked upon and our hands have handled." This is suggestive of a progressive revelation. What you have heard is the promise of your possession, you must see with your eyes of understanding before your hand can handle it. Vision is the ability to see. It is having access to a divine program. In the book of Numbers, God had already told them, "I will give you Canaan". However Moses needed eyes. In Numbers 14, he sent out 12 spies to spy out the land. In Joshua 2:1, Joshua did the same thing. There is power in spying out what you want to possess.

Do not be led by the opinions of men. You can't step into a business without spying it out. It doesn't matter if an Angel appeared to you; maybe Jesus Himself appeared to you and said you must do Computer Engineering. If you jump into it without spying it out you may fail. It is true God told you, but there is wisdom and power in spying out. Make enquiries and get some solid facts, like David Oyedepo says, "facts make fat".

Proverbs 29:18, "Where there is no vision, the people perish..." People perish because God will not do anything you have not yet seen. Seeing connotes understanding. It is what you thoroughly understand that you will see and that in turn determines what manifestations you will have. The extent to which you can see determines how much you can possess. God told Abraham "... Lift up now thine eyes, and look from the place where thou art northward, and southward, and eastward and westward: For all the land which thou seest, to thee will I give it, and to thy seed forever." He did not stop there. He then said, "Arise and walk."

What you have not seen, you cannot conquer. The place you don't know, the place you don't spy out, you cannot overcome. The Psalmist said, "The Lord is my Shepherd", the wise shepherd already knows ahead of time where the good pasture is because often, he has gone to spy it out before taking the sheep there. No matter how your vision was delivered to you; it doesn't just jump up into place, Moses sent people to spy out the land that they were going, and Joshua did the same thing. He took time to get details of the vision. Spying spiritually is the cure for frustration from which many people suffer; it is true they got a genuine vision for that business, but they did not take time to spy it out and understand what it entails in order to locate a strategy.

After Joshua spied out the land, he devised a strategy for taking the land. He attacked the land in the middle and Jericho was conquered, he moved to the south and then moved to the north. He had a strategy.

Meditation: The Good Or The Best
Oswald Chambers
Genesis 13:8-18

As soon as you begin to live the life of faith in God, fascinating and physically gratifying possibilities will open up before you. These things are yours by right, but if you are living the life of faith you will exercise your right to waive your rights, and let God make your choice for you. God sometimes allows you to get into a place of testing where your own welfare would be the appropriate thing to consider, if you were not living the life of faith. But if you are, you will joyfully waive your right and allow God to make your choice for you. This is the discipline God uses to transform the natural into the spiritual through obedience to his voice.

Whenever our right becomes the guiding factor of our lives, it dulls our spiritual insight. The greatest enemy of the life of faith in God is not sin, but good choices, which are not quite good enough. The good is always the enemy of the best. In this passage, it would seem that the wisest thing in the world for Abram to do would be to choose. It was his right, and the people around him would consider him to be a fool for not choosing.

Many of us do not continue to grow spiritually because we prefer to choose on the basis of our rights, instead of relying on God to make the choice for us. We have to learn to walk according to the standard which has its eyes focused on God. And as God says to us, as he did to Abram,

"...walk before me..."
(Genesis 17:1)

Be conscious that the greatest discernment we need is to know what God has called us into, and where He wants us to be. Are you in a wrong business right now, because you accepted an appointment and then discovered it is a wrong place for you? You need courage to relocate yourself to the right place where God has called you. Prayer and fasting abusing the devil, are not sufficient on their own, you must take practical steps. There are some people who are not called to do the business of selling because they will give everything away; they are too sentimental. Some others are not called to be in the service industry because their face never wears a smile. So, when someone enters their restaurant for instance, they leave well fed but dissatisfied - "the food is good but that proprietor is unfriendly".

If you are where God has called you, don't be distracted and don't be discouraged. Don't also allow success stories of other people in their own business to derail you because even when you are in the perfect will of God, you will have challenges and problems, you will still fight attacks of the devil.

No matter how great your vision, you will need to work, because work is a gift to release and realize your vision. In Ecclesiastes 5:19 the bible calls work a gift from God but many people see work as punishment. No matter the vision, if you don't like work, and you don't enjoy working, you may never shine because work is the gift that God has given us to enable us to possess what is inside our vision. When God made Adam in the Garden of Eden, the bible says, "He gave him to till the garden." He gave him work. When God Himself had a vision, for a garden, He did not wish it, He did not confess it He planted it. God did not prophecy a garden. So work is the gift that fulfills your vision. Planting is indicative of some form of work.

A man of God said 70% of people never discover what God has assigned for them because opportunity always disguises itself as work and most people don't accomplish their vision and destiny because opportunity disguised itself as work. So whenever you dodge the work, you actually dodge your destiny. Robert Collyer, the blacksmith preacher had this to say: "My life is divided into two sections - forty years in the pulpit, twenty-one years at the anvil. I have worked on long lines, and I will say to young men that, when your homes and your schools have done all they can for you, and you begin the work of life, you must take hold with a will and be content to work hard on long lines. People say that such and such a person has genius for what he or she takes in hand, and that is the secret of the success attained. But I say that genius means strong devotion and steadfast application. You may imagine that you can go from the bottom to the top of the ladder at one jump, but it is not true. Going up the ladder at one jump is like the toy monkey that goes up at a jump and comes down headfirst. The men and women who achieve true success are all hard climbers. They work in one direction. Our course must not be like a cow-path, all over the pasture and into the woods, for that may mean through the woods into the wilderness."

David Oyedepo's conclusion on this matter is quite simple he says, "When you do nothing, you are harming your destiny. When you understand that work is a gift, then you will realise that God is actually your employer. You are working not in order to be paid; you are working for God to make you. So when you do nothing, you are destroying your destiny."

There is no one that God called into His work, who was not hard working and doing something on their own before their calling. When you understand the mystery of work, you will understand that God is your employer and until He finds you serious and ready to work, your vision may never be released to you. Don't dodge the responsibility of work; don't see any work as below you. Great fortunes are largely disguised in low estates.

A man, who studied banking and finance, shared this testimony in church. He had looked everywhere for a job, but every bank he applied to rejected him. One day, he saw an application for the post of a motorcar driver in a bank. He said he advised himself, and concluded that, "half bread is better than none, I have this certificate, I can't eat it, but I have this driver's license that may provide food for my family." So he applied. And as he was standing with the drivers to be interviewed, one of the managers passing by looked at him and said, "Please excuse me, what are you doing here?" He replied that he was waiting for the interview. The manager took a good look at him and said, "I am not sure you should be here please follow me." Coincidentally they were also interviewing assistant managers that day but that position was never advertised, so if he were waiting for a vacancy ad, he would never have known the position was available. People within the bank brought their own candidates. The General Manager who saw him standing with the drivers thought he had missed his way because of the way he was dressed. He then took him by the hand and said, you don't belong here. When they arrived where they were interviewing assistant managers, the other managers all assumed that he was the General Manager's candidate and he got the job as assistant manager. Why? Because God saw his heart, he was ready to work as a driver. If he were not ready to work, his destiny would not have been released.

Meditation: The example of God's adornment
Clement of Rome

"What must we do, then, my brothers? Should we relax our efforts at well doing, and cease to exercise Christian love? God forbid that we, at least, should ever come to such a pass. On the contrary, let us be earnestly, even passionately, eager to set about any kind of activity that is good."

Even the architect and Lord of the universe himself takes a delight in working. In his supreme power he has established the heavens, and in his unsearchable wisdom set them in order. He divided the earth from the waters around it, and settled it securely on the firm foundation of his will, and at his word he called to life the beasts of the field that roam its surface. He formed the sea and its creatures, and confined them by his power. Above all, with his own sacred and immaculate hands he fashioned man, who in virtue of his intelligence is the chiefest and greatest of all his works and the very likeness of his own image; for God said, "Let us make man in our image after our likeness; and let them have dominion over the fish of the sea, and over the fowl of the air, and over the cattle and over all the earth, and over every creeping thing upon the earth. So God created man in his own image, in the image of God created he him, male and female he created them" (Genesis 1:26-27). And when he had made an end of all his works, he gave them his approval and his blessing, saying, increase and multiply (Genesis 1:28).

We see, then, that good works have not only embellished the lives of all just men, but are an adornment with which even the Lord has delighted to deck himself; and therefore, with such an example before us, let us spare no effort to obey his will, and put all our energies into the work of righteousness.

CHAPTER THREE

THE LAW OF PREPARATION

Joshua 1:11 says "Prepare".

The person God will use is the one who has prepared. It takes preparation to prosper. "So Jotham became mighty, because he prepared his ways before the Lord, his God." 2 Chronicles 27:6

If you don't prepare, you will never be ready for the reality of what your vision entails; it may look so great, but when you step in, you will see that things are not as rosy. It always demands adequate preparation. Joshua was well prepared for his assignment. He followed Moses, studied him and submitted to him. He did all that was necessary for him to take up the business. Now ask yourself a question, if you were God, would you choose yourself to do the particular business you desire now? Be honest with God and with yourself. If you choose to be the manager of a bank for instance and you feel "I can do it, I can do all things," but you lack the relevant skill and experience, you won't last one week. You will crack up, because you don't have the adequate skill and maturity to handle the assignment.

In Psalms 1:3 the Bible says,

> *"And he shall be like a tree planted by the rivers of water, that bringeth forth his fruit in his season; his leaf also shall not wither; and whatsoever he doeth shall prosper."*

In the natural, a tree doesn't grow overnight. Before a tree will get to the point that it starts to bring forth fruits, it necessarily must send its root down, obtain some stability and some maturity and then fruits will begin to grow.

In business, there are few instant successes and many times those who are instant successes don't last long because they have not acquired the maturity to sustain success. Preparation is important. If you can pay the price of endurance and faith, you will not succeed. Joshua followed Moses and learnt everything that was to be learned. Elisha followed Elijah and he understood everything about that business and he did greater things than Elijah did. If you are more concerned about comfort than preparation, you can never fulfill your vision. If you are focused on your vision, you will take enough time to persevere and prepare.

Samuel Griswold Goodrich said,

> *"Perseverance gives power to weakness, and opens to poverty the world's wealth. It spreads fertility over the barren landscape, and bids the choicest fruits and flowers spring up and flourish in the desert abode of thorns and briers."*

God called Bishop David Oyedepo on May 1, 1981 and when the vision was delivered, it lasted 18 hours. He did not just jump out and say, "God just spoke to me for 18 hours." He spent another 26 months praying, fasting, planning and "spying" before the ministry started. There was no office when he eventually started, but a disciplined attitude towards work forbade his team to sit idle; they resumed on the first day, seated around a table tennis board. In those early days, they worked out a master plan for every department of the ministry. They did not have a motor cycle, but they already had administrative procedures for a transport department. Twenty years later the transport department took delivery of 87 passenger buses in one day, fully bought and paid for. We need time to prepare, to grow and we also need time to change. Don't be discouraged by where you are now. Maybe the business you are in doesn't look like you are achieving your aim now, please don't be discouraged because God is not so much interested in you having some respect among your contemporaries as He is in developing your character. He is not in a hurry to make you a quick success that fizzles out under pressure.

When God succeeds in developing your character he will give you a base in that business that will enable you to overtake those who have gone ahead ten years before you. Let me explain one or two advantages of preparation. If you are prepared, you will avoid the mistake of biting off more than you can chew. Many people due to lack of preparation often wander out of their primary calling. They just jump inside any door that opens, and often it's a wrong door so they crash and miss the real door to their fulfillment. God will correct every error of your life.

One of the greatest challenges in business, is not just locating a vision, it is not just locating what to do, but knowing when to move fast and when to slow down: when to move quickly on a particular idea and when to slow down in carrying it out. The truth is that sometimes, in order not to make major financial mistakes, you need to go on your knees and pray. You must have faith and common sense. If you move ahead too fast and your cash flow cannot sustain the vision, even though it is a vision from the Lord, you may crash. You need faith and common sense.

> *"Through wisdom is a house builded; and by knowledge it is established: And by understanding shall the chambers be filled with all precious and pleasant riches."*
> Proverbs 24:3

But what do you do in order to move with God? God gave Joshua the boundaries of his vision but Joshua never tried to take all at once. Prayerfully, he took it one step at a time. Every step you take prepares you for the next step. So preparation never ends. Praise God! Prayer is essential in making your vision happen. That is the only way you can know the details and specific direction to take each time.

Bishop David Oyedepo shared with us how on the day he was commissioned into ministry on 17th September 1983, everyone prayed concerning the city of Jos in Nigeria because he had told everyone "God is sending me to Jos." But on the final night, he packed his bags and decided to seek the Lord for final instructions. While praising God, God said to him, "remember about 5 years ago when you were on holiday in Jos with your cousin, you desired in your heart to settle down in this town." God then told him "you heard yourself not me." It is true I called you, but as regards the location of your assignment, you only heard yourself, not me." This demonstrates the need for spiritual sensitivity, if he didn't go back to pray, the ministry might not be where it is now. Maybe the vision would have died in Jos.

He went back and suffered the shame, because everybody began to look at him and thought, "Look at this man that we prayed for, he said he was going to Jos, is he a deceiver?" God said, "I will make you see the price of not hearing me very well," and Bishop Oyedepo must have said, "Lord whatever the price is, I will gladly pay it to hear you correctly." Then one day while in prayer with his wife, as he was asking God for direction, he opened his Bible to the Book of Acts 9:6 and he read the scripture where Jesus said, "Go into the city, and it shall be told thee what thou must do." And immediately the Holy Ghost ignited his understanding. In Nigeria at that time, there was religious persecution against Christians in Kaduna. Saul was going to Damascus to persecute the Christians, so Kaduna must be the Nigerian Damascus to which God was assigning him. The Bishop said, as he closed his Bible he knew that prayer time was over, it was time to go to Damascus; and that is how the ministry started in Kaduna. It is only in prayer that you can get fine details and get the divine strategy for succeeding in your business. One wise man said, pray as if the whole success of your business depends completely on God, but work as if the success of that business depends completely on you. Preparation will instill strength and courage. Spy out, prepare and pray, then strength and courage will come.

God does not just want to bless us. In the process of blessing us, He also wants to change us, He wants to mature us, to strengthen us, so that by the time we achieve the fullness of His blessing we will be strong enough to sustain that blessing.
There are areas of change and preparation in our personal development that are important to our success.

1. Your Appearance: The way you appear is a message to people around you.

American philosopher Ralph Waldo Emerson once said, "The sense of being perfectly dressed gives us a feeling of inward tranquility which religion is powerless to bestow." If you are in business, the way you appear in your business shows your respect for that business. How you respect your business, is how people will respond to it. In Genesis 41, a miracle happened to Joseph. He was called out of the prison, his vision was about to be fulfilled but he was not careless, he was sensitive to his environment.

> *"Then Pharaoh sent and called Joseph, and they brought him hastily out of the dungeon: and he shaved himself, and changed his raiment, and came in unto Pharaoh"*
> Genesis 41:14

Joseph not only had the gift of interpretation of dreams; he also had practical wisdom. The Egyptians were not cattle breeders; rather they were clean-shaven city builders while the Jews by tradition were nomadic cattle traders with characteristic long beards. When Joseph was told that Pharaoh was looking for him, he did not rush into Pharaoh's presence. He said, "Wait, let me prepare myself to appear in his presence." He created an atmosphere of acceptance around himself. Pharaoh looked at Joseph, and his clean and neat appearance must have contributed to his exaltation to the post of the governor of Egypt. It was not only Joseph's gift that made a way for him; his appearance also spoke for him. In Genesis 41:14, the Bible says "and he shaved himself." There is no useless passage in the Holy Scriptures. The Holy Ghost included this part to let us know the importance of our appearance. To Pharaoh, Joseph looked like one of his own people. Some Christians think erroneously that they are in the world but they are not of this world, so they look wretched and tattered, yet they pray and fast and speak in tongues to get a job. Someone claims that they have the Holy Ghost, but the hair on their head is so dirty, and their armpit is stinking. They forget the popular adage that cleanliness is next to godliness.

Your appearance will affect the business of your life. It is only God who sees the heart; that is why con men cheat many people. If a dishonest person can deceive people by dressing well, then imagine what success you will achieve if you are honest and well dressed?

THE LAW OF PREPARATION

God wants you to create a climate of acceptability. If you contrast Proverbs 7:10, where the Bible talks about the woman with the attire of a harlot, and Proverbs 31:22, where the Bible talks about the attire of the virtuous woman you will see two distinct women. One is clearly described as virtuous by the way she appeared and the other was called a prostitute this. Some women are never respected even though they are married because of the way they appear. "The apparel oft proclaims the man," said William Shakespeare. "An emperor in his nightcap," says Goldsmith "would not meet with half the respect of an emperor with a crown."

The late archbishop Benson Idahosa said, "You are addressed, the way you dress" (people will speak to you the way they see you). He also said, "you address the way you are dressed." If you are wearing a suit and somebody just crashes into your car, you won't get down and remove your suit and start fighting; at least you will respect yourself. But if you are wearing a pair of shorts, you may be provoked into an unruly act. So you also carry yourself according to the way you are dressed. Similarly your appearance and the appearance of your business premises will dictate the pace and the success of your business. Some people turn their business premises into a social club, a free for all bar where everyone with nothing to do can while away time. That business can never succeed. It has become a gossip arena where those who have nothing to do exercise their jaws. You must create an appearance of diligence and purposefulness so that immediately someone enters your premises; the atmosphere and disposition should communicate to your potential client, industry, sincerity, dignity and prudence.

2. Your Understanding: Begin to increase your understanding of your work.

Whatever your business is, strive to understand the details more because your success is determined by the problems you can solve in that business. You can't make progress beyond your ability to provide solutions for people and you can't solve problems beyond your level of understanding. So improve yourself. Educate yourself and look for personal counseling from people who are in your discipline. Read books, look for magazines, attend business seminars and increase your knowledge.

3. Your Behaviour: This includes your attitude towards people.

Everything you do or say creates an atmosphere around you. You must watch the state of your mind because your attitude either attracts business to you or sends business away from you. If you can create an atmosphere of integrity, peace, stability and friendliness, people will enjoy you first and then they will enjoy doing business with you, and your success will be guaranteed.

> *"And Abel, he also brought of the firstlings of his flock and of the fat thereof. And the Lord had respect unto Abel and to his offering"*
> *Genesis 4:4*

The person of Abel found favour before his offering was acceptable to God. If you can cultivate a pleasant personality that is affable, people will enjoy your persona and then appreciate what you have to offer.

THE LAW OF PREPARATION

Meditation: Cardinal Rules For Business Success

Charles B. Rouss, who was once penniless, walking the streets day and night, eating at free lunch counters and sleeping at police stations, attained great heights of successful achievement as a multi-millionaire merchant on New York's Broadway.

Mr. Rouss gives us his cardinal rules for business success. These rules for a successful life could well be carried in the pocket book of every young man and woman throughout the world:

1. *Keep good company or none.*
2. *Never be idle. If your hands cannot be fully employed, attend to the cultivation of your mind.*
3. *Always speak the truth. Make few promises. Live up to your engagements.*
4. *Keep your own secrets if you have any.*
5. *When you speak to a person, look him in the face.*
6. *Good company and good conversation are the very sinews of virtue.*
7. *Good character is above all things. Your character cannot be essentially injured, except by your own acts. If anyone speaks evil of you let your life be so that none will believe him. Keep yourself innocent, if you would be happy.*
8. *Drink no kind of intoxicating liquors.*
9. *Live within your income.*
10. *When you retire, think over what you have been doing during the day.*
11. *Never play at a game of chance.*
12. *Avoid temptation through fear that you may not withstand it.*
13. *Earn money before you spend it. Never run into debt unless you see your way out of it again. Never borrow if you can possibly avoid it.*
14. *Do not marry until you are able to support a wife.*

15. *Never speak evil of anyone.*
16. *Be just before you are generous.*
17. *Save when you are young to spend when you are old.*
18. *Read over the above maxims at least once a week.*

CHAPTER FOUR

THE LAW OF OBEDIENCE

In Joshua 4:9, Joshua built a memorial on the banks of River Jordan. The erection of that set of stones was a direct commandment from God. In Joshua 5:2-5, Joshua took the people through the covenant of circumcision at Gilgal, the sign of the Abrahamic covenant that spiritually indicated the putting to death the deeds of the flesh by the spirit, here God rolled away the reproach of Egypt and consecrated the people to Himself. This was also in direct obedience to the Lord. In the sixth chapter of the book of Joshua, the walls of Jericho came down by divine instruction, a clear demonstration that spiritual victories are won by means and upon principles that may be foolish in the view of the world but backed by divine authority.

These three events in chapters 4, 5, and 6, point to "The law of obedience". When Israel arrived in the promised land, after they had crossed Jordan, they confronted the first and the strongest city called Jericho and God told Joshua, "I will give you this city but everything you recover there is mine." This is a type of the law of first fruits:

MAXIMISING BUSINESS ADVANTAGE - THE JOSHUA REVELATION

> *"And the city shall be accursed, even it, and all that are therein, to the Lord; only Rahab the harlot shall live, she and all who are with her in the house, because she hid the messengers that we sent. And ye, in any wise keep yourselves from the accursed thing, lest ye make yourselves accursed… But all the silver, and gold, and vessels of brass and iron, are consecrated unto the Lord; they shall come into the treasury of the Lord"*
> Joshua 6: 17-19.

They thought they had obeyed, but in chapter 7, they fought with a small town called Ai and they suffered a great defeat, because Achan had broken the law of obedience to the first fruits. God said, "every other city you conquer, you can take the spoils, but this first one you will not overcome by your strength, I will give you the victory. It will not be by your expertise but by my Spirit, however you must come back to recognize me as the one who gave you the city"(Paraphrased). Did they fight to win Jericho? No! They shouted and a wall wide enough for chariot races fell down flat. That was the power of God. What happened to Achan, The man who disobeyed the law of first fruits? His wife, an innocent woman who knew nothing, was punished and also all his children, innocent little children, were all stoned to death and burnt in the valley of Achor. There is reward for obedience, and there are grave consequences for disobedience. There is no testimony in this kingdom without obedience. Obedience is the key to abundance with God because, He relates to man based on His covenant. "…My covenant will I not break, nor alter the thing that is gone out of my lips"

Psalm 89:34 God said
"…I have exalted my words above my name."

In other words God is saying, even I, cannot disobey what I have said. If you can locate what God said and tell Him, "God you said in your word, this is written concerning me…" just be assured that your prayer is answered because God abides faithful

THE LAW OF OBEDIENCE

He cannot deny Himself.

> *"Acquaint now thyself with him, and be at peace; thereby good shall come unto thee. Receive I pray thee, the law from his mouth, and lay up his words in thine heart"*
> *Job 22:21*

Jesus is called the prince of peace. The degree of your acquaintance with Him and your level of obedience to Him determine your peace. Thereby through the process of acquaintance good comes to you because

> *"every good and perfect gift is from above."*
> *James 1:17*

Receive I pray thee the law from His mouth. Receive it and lay it up in your heart so you can obey it.

> *"If thou return to the Almighty, thou shalt be built up; thou shalt put away iniquity very far from thy tents. Then shalt thou lay up gold as dust, and the gold of Ophir as the stones of the brooks."*
> *Job 22:24*

Then, and not before then, shalt thou lay up gold as dust. Yea! The Almighty shall be the defense of the gold He brings to you even though it's like dust. He will not allow the devil to touch it. The Almighty becomes your defense and your protection. He will bless you and protect that blessing. That is your portion from this day in Jesus name. God instructs us to receive from Him his wisdom that contains life. He said as long as you keep returning to me, you shall be built up.

> *"Except the Lord builds a house, they labour in vain that build it"* Ps 127:1.

Except you return to Him who is the builder of all things, you cannot be built up. You can try in your own strength but you can never be built up without the hand of God. There is a law that you must return to. It is the law of tithing in willful obedience. It is a non-negotiable and a non-transferable responsibility. You can't step in for your wife or your husband. If you don't return, you cannot be built up. If you lay up His words and receive that law, you will lay up gold as dust.

"if you are willing and obedient, you shall eat the good of the land."
Isaiah 1:19

But it is not just any kind of obedience that is acceptable unto God. A coerced obedience is not accepted. It must be a willing obedience. Obedience from the heart is what counts not because you are forced.

"if they obey and serve Him, they shall spend their days in prosperity, and their years in pleasure".
Job 36:11

In other words, as far as God is concerned, prosperity and a pleasurable life are a function of your willful obedience.

In 2 Corinthians 8:12 Paul said,
"For if there be first a willing mind, it is accepted…"

Whatever you do, God first looks at your willingness. The law of obedience is the law of willful obedience. You can only willfully obey God after you have realized that God is God and there is no one like Him. When you understand His weight and worth, your willingness will be engaged. This kingdom is a kingdom of covenants. That is why you have the Old and the New covenant. A testament is also called a covenant. So if you don't understand covenant, you cannot succeed in a kingdom that is ruled by covenant. Financial abundance is a function of covenant; your obedience to a certain law, the law of giving and receiving. Until you recognize your responsibility in giving, you may never enjoy the benefit of receiving because a covenant is an agreement binding on two parties. There is a covenantee and covenantor and they both have responsibilities. Until your own responsibility is fulfilled, there is no access for God to fulfil His own responsibility in your life, no matter how much He wants to do it.

Deuteronomy 8:18,

"thou shalt remember the Lord thy God: for it is He who giveth thee power to get wealth".

In other words there is something called "power to get wealth" and by the mercy of God, by the Spirit of understanding that power will be released into your life. You cannot die poor in the midst of plenty. There is enough in this world for everyone, but poverty is in every country. Poverty doesn't respect anybody. If you don't respect the law of God, poverty won't respect you. But I see poverty bow to you as you embrace this law. The answer is in the Bible. The answer is not abroad but in the covenant. God is not a respecter of colour. The largest church building in the world built debt free is in Nigeria pastored by Bishop David Oyedepo, the Faith Tabernacle.

The late archbishop Benson Idahosa said, a lizard in Cameroon won't get to France and become an alligator but if you are an alligator in Cameroon, when you get to France, you will still be an alligator. So better learn how to be an alligator where you are. Bishop David Oyedepo said, "The answer is not abroad; the answer is "in-broad." If you will allow the word of God to broaden your mind, everything abroad will come to you. That verse in Deuteronomy 8 says the power to get wealth is a function of an established covenant between God and you. If you will enter that covenant, the power to get wealth will be yours. In Genesis 8:22, God says that as long as this earth remains, seedtime and harvest shall not cease. As long as you see day and night, then seedtime and harvest time cannot stop.

In other words, giving is actually an act of sowing. Whatever you give, is a seed you sow into your own destiny and future. Whatever you sow or give never leaves your life. As long as there's day and night, it's in your life.

In 2 Corinthians 9:10, Paul made a very profound statement. "Now he that minister seed to the sower both minister bread for your food and multiply your seed sown." In other words, prosperity in your business and wealth in your life is only a function of the multiplied effect by God of the seeds you have sown. He said He would multiply the seed you sow. He doesn't multiply prayers. Can you imagine going to a farm somewhere and then believe that because you are very anointed you can prophesy potatoes to fill the place. You can pray from now till December, do you think potatoes will materialize there? No! God gave a law; it is called the law of seed propagation.

Genesis 1:12
"And the earth brought forth grass, and herb yielding seed after it's kind, and the tree yielding fruit, whose seed was in itself, after its kind: and God saw that it was good."

He said everything would have their seed in themselves. In other words maybe you are not married now but your children are inside you. You are carrying the seed that will produce them. Your future, your destiny is with you now. God will not do anything in your life in the future that He has not already given you a seed for.

Everything you are looking for is already inside you. What will give you a divine breakthrough in your life is already with you. Zechariah 8:12 says, "For the seed shall be prosperous…" It is the seed that determines prosperity. It is what you do with seed available to you that determines your future, what you have done with what you had before is what has determined where you are now. He only multiplies the seeds sown. In other words, if there are no seeds sown, there is nothing for God to multiply or prosper.

2 Corinthians 9:6-8

> *"But this I say, He that soweth sparingly shall reap also sparingly; and he who soweth bountifully shall reap bountifully. Every man according as he purposeth in his heart, so let him give, not grudgingly, or of necessity; for God loveth a cheerful giver. And God is able to make all grace abound toward you, that ye, always having all sufficiency in all things, may abound to every good work."*

This is a law that demands practical obedience. It doesn't respect anybody whether you are a Pastor or an Apostle. If you don't sow, there is nothing God will multiply. In other words, from this scripture, there is a life we can live with God where an understanding of this law of giving will make all grace to abound to us. That always, we will have all sufficiency in all things.

Abraham entered that domain with God. He was not a Pastor, he was a businessman, and he was in the cattle business yet in Genesis 24:1, the Bible says *"Abraham became old and well stricken in age and God had blessed Abraham in all things;"* including old age and good health. All grace abounded towards him in all sufficiency in all things. In Isaiah 51:1-3, the Bible says "you that follow after righteousness, look unto Abraham your father, look unto the hole of the pit from which you are dug, look unto Sarah who bore you, for God called him alone. It says God desires to comfort you. He desires to make the wasted seasons of your life like the Garden of Eden."(Paraphrased)

God's desire is for your life to be like that of Abraham; blessed in all things. In fact Paul told us in the book of Galatians 3:13-

14 that Christ has redeemed us from the curse of the law, that the blessings of Abraham might become ours. That shows how powerful the blessings of Abraham were.

But how did Abraham get to this realm? In Genesis 12, God told Abraham, "leave where you are, leave your brethren, get out of your country, get out of the familiar traditions." All you know about business is borrowing and you have borrowed until you are borrowed out. Some people just believe that business is synonymous with borrowing. God said get out of that tradition, I have a better way, follow my own way and Abraham obeyed, he departed. He obeyed because he believed God.

This obedience brought him great wealth in Genesis 13:2, the Bible says, *"And Abraham was very rich in cattle, in silver and in gold"*. By Genesis 14:20, he paid tithes of all. *"And blessed be the most high God, which hath delivered thine enemies into thy hand. And he gave him tithes of all."*

By Genesis 22 after he demonstrated his understanding of the law of tithing he entered a higher dimension of relationship with God, the realm of sacrifice. He gave a fearful sacrifice that connected human generations after him into a covenant of blessing forever. By Genesis 24:1, God had blessed him in all things. The first revelation of giving God showed Abraham was tithing. Until you understand tithing, your life will remain tight. No matter how big your business is, you must understand tithing. In Hebrews 7, you will discover that when you pay your tithes, you are not giving to the Pastor or the church. The Bible says, Jesus Himself is the one that collects the tithes, because He is our High Priest in heaven, He is the one who receives it from you and represents you before God. He says to the Father, *"this man is still on our register for help, for abundance, and for protection."*

THE LAW OF OBEDIENCE

Hebrews 7:1-8,

"For this Melchisedec, king of Salem, priest of the most high God, who met Abraham returning from the slaughter of the kings, and blessed him; To whom also Abraham gave a tenth part of all; first being by interpretation King of righteousness, and after that also King of Salem, which is, King of peace; Without father, without mother, without descent, having neither beginning of days, nor end of life; but made like unto the Son of God; abideth a priest continually.
Now consider how great this man was, unto whom even the patriarch Abraham gave he tenth of the spoils. And verily they that are of the sons of Levi, who receive the office of the priesthood, have a commandment to take tithes of the people according to the law, that is, of their brethren, though they came out of the loins of Abraham: But whose descent is not counted from them received tithes of Abraham, and blessed him that had the promises. And without all contradiction the less is blessed of the better. And here men that die receive tithes; but there he receiveth them of whom it is witnessed that he liveth".

The tithe is the first tenth of your increase (1/10). Melchisedec, the Bible tells us is a type of Jesus Christ. It was Jesus who met Abraham and to whom Abraham gave a tenth part of all. The Bible says in 2 Corinthians 5:21 that Jesus became sin that we might become the righteousness of God in Him. So He is the King of kings who made us righteous by bringing us into His righteousness. He is also the king of Salem, which is king of peace and Isaiah 9:6 tells us He shall be called the Prince of Peace. When John the beloved encountered Jesus Christ in the Book of Revelations He told John, *"I am Alpha and Omega, the beginning and the end."* This aptly matches the description of Melchisedec, "Without Father, without mother without descent having neither beginning, nor end of life, but made like unto the Son of God, abideth a priest continually."

Why would Abraham the Patriarch who had the promise, give all the tithe of the spoils of war? Because, the tithe is the connection to the eternal blessings of God. When you pay your tithes, it's not for the Pastor because the pastor too, if he doesn't pay his tithe, will experience a closed heaven, as things will become tight for him. No matter who you are, you are disconnected from heaven's supplies when you don't pay your tithes. That is why in Mal 3:7-12 God said, "Even from the days of your fathers ye are gone away from mine ordinances (laws) and have not kept them. Return unto me and I will return to you saith the Lord of Hosts (until you return I can't return). But you said, Wherein shall we return? Will a man rob God? Yet you have robbed me. But ye say wherein have we robbed thee? In tithes and offerings. Ye are cursed with a curse: for ye have robbed me, even this whole nation. Bring ye all the tithes into the storehouse, that there may be meat in mine house, and prove me now herewith, saith the Lord of hosts, if I will not open you the windows of heaven and pour you out a blessing, that there shall not be room enough to receive it. And I will rebuke the devourer for your sakes, and he shall not destroy the fruits of your ground; neither shall your vine cast her fruit before the time in the field, saith the Lord of hosts. And all nations shall call you blessed: for ye shall be a delightsome land, saith the Lord of hosts.

Listen, tithe is not a seed you sow, it's not your own. If it's your own, God won't say you are robbing Him, your tithe belongs to God. It is God's portion of your increase. God says my son I give you ten but return one to me to show that you still want your name on my register for blessings. He said acknowledge me as the giver of all things, without me, you can do nothing. God is the only helper of man. If anybody helps you it's because God moved His heart to help you. If you think it's your power that got that contract or that increase, you will soon see just how powerful you are when He withdraws His presence.

The most foolish thing is to disregard the laws of God. It is even more foolish to look at God in the face and to say, "God you should understand I need all of the ten portions now." And that is what many business people do. They make an investment and then money comes in and they become so excited that they begin to make all kinds of wild calculations. He looks at five hundred thousand dollars and says, "God wait, let me turn over this money up to five million dollars then I will pay the tithe of the five million and also the tithe of that other five hundred thousand." God then withdraws His presence and then everything goes wrong. When things become difficult, then he begins to pray and fast. May things not go wrong for you in Jesus name. Amen. It is the devil that corrupts the mind of man and deceives man from the riches of God's inheritance that is accessible by simple obedience.

You can have two people receive the same amount of money and go to the same market and one has paid his tithes and has ninety percent in his pocket. The other man has his hundred percent. The first man spends 90% and buys goods worth 120%, this man enters the marketplace with 90% that has touched the hands of Jesus, and that 90% supernaturally has purchasing power of 120% while the other man with his 100% cannot get more than 70% worth, now, who has gained? This is exactly what tithing is about. It puts the blessings of God upon what you have. Don't begin to turn God's law around in your mind. Many people have failed because they have tried to reason out God's instruction. God cannot change. Don't try to reason it out. It is foolishness to implore God to understand that the children are going back to school and there is no food in the house. Lord, let me use this tithe now and later I will pay it. You may never be able to pay back. You know why? In Malachi 3:9, the Bible says when you withhold your tithe from God you come under a curse. When a man curses you, you can pray and break that curse, but when God curses you, who will pray with you to break the curse?

What is the effect of the curse of the law?

In Mark 11:20-21, we see the effect of the curse of the law. The Bible said the tree that Jesus cursed began to wither from the root. *"And in the morning, as they passed by, they saw the fig tree dried up from the roots. And Peter calling to remembrance saith unto him, Master, behold, the fig tree which thou cursedst is withered away."*

When you see someone in business and the business is withering away everyday, he naturally holds the finances tighter saying, No! It's too small; a tithe cannot come out of this one. He keeps going down, withering from the roots. The place from where he could draw help and strength from is the place that he locks up tight. Peter said the fig tree, which you cursed, has withered. When a business is withering while the owner struggles and refuses to sleep struggling day and night, with nothing to show? The business may be under a curse. It is not the devil and it's not witchcraft working against him, he has put himself under the curse of God. When God withdraws, the devil has all access.

Whether you like it or not, everybody pays this tithe, call it ground rent if you will. You either pay willingly to the right source or you pay unwillingly through the devourer in a wrong way, either through hospital bills or through accidents or to thieves and robbers. You must pay all the same. My prayer is that you will not pay in the wrong way anymore in the name of Jesus.

Everybody pays. You think the Pastor wants your money? Okay! You will give it to the devil if you don't understand how to give it to God. That's the truth. Many have started well, where are they now? Ask them how their capital disappeared they can't explain it. But they are on the ground now. Why? When the devourer comes to collect, he never collects 10%, which is why he is called the devourer. He enters and collects more than is due, and what he cannot collect, he will waste, and he will scatter. Your future will not be scattered if you simply obey.

In Luke 16:11, Jesus said,

> *"If therefore ye have not been faithful in the unrighteous mammon, who will commit to your trust the true riches?"*

Your tithe insures your life. It is an insurance against sickness, failure, accidents and evil. Jesus was saying if you therefore have not been faithful with money, who will commit to your trust the true riches; long life, sickness free-life, frustration free-life, failure free-life, depression free-life, a life where at His right hand there are pleasures for ever more. If you are not faithful with the unrighteous money, i.e. God gives you ten and says take nine and return one back to me, to acknowledge me, to thank me. Even though I have used men to bless you, you should know this blessing is coming from me. You begin to give excuses and even promise to double the tithe by the next business, because you need plenty of money. I look at some people and I pity their lack of understanding. They say "Pastor, you need to understand, in our business, that is how we do it. I want to quickly re-invest. Later they will come and say, "You know pastor, please pray for me for the money I re-invested to yield fruit." What God calls True Riches cannot be bought with money. In other words, your tithes do two things:

1. *It insures your life against calamities.*

If you have paid your tithe, God will ensure that what you have acknowledged Him with is not used to acknowledge sickness or to pay accident bills in the hospital, He won't allow thieves to steal your goods. He said, "I will rebuke the devourer." The devil is going up and down seeking whom he may destroy. When he comes around you, God lifts a standard against him and says, " that man is registered with me". Your tithe is like a Passover ensign that will make evil "Passover" your business.

2. It gives you access to what Jesus calls true Riches.

True riches are things that money cannot buy: peace, safety, protection, favor and long life. To be free from depressions, to get up in the morning and are full of joy because everything around you is just fine. Some people have plenty of money but plenty of problems and depression. God will give you true riches from today in the name of Jesus Christ. It's up to you. In Psalm 20 we see a type of what Joshua did when they built a memorial before the Lord in the midst of Jordan. The Bible explains to us that our offering builds a memorial of remembrance for us. In the day you cry to God, He will remember how you have appeared before Him in the past. Let me give you two instances in the Bible. The first is in Mathew 5:23, Jesus said "if you bring your gift to the altar..." In other words, when you come to God, God expects you to come with a gift. Jesus was still upholding this law because God gave that law in Deuteronomy16:16 He said *"let none of the children of Israel appear before me empty,"* why? When you come before God, it is your offering that represents you. In the Old Testament, when they came with sheep and goats, it represented them. God said never appear before me empty. To come to God and say I don't have is to come under a curse.

THE LAW OF OBEDIENCE

Meditation: God's Great Delight
Mathew Henry. 1 Samuel 15: 10-23

Here we are plainly told... that humble, sincere, and conscientious obedience to the will of God is more pleasing and acceptable to him than all burnt offerings and sacrifices. A careful conformity to moral precepts recommends us to God more than all ceremonial observances (see Micah 6:6-8; Hosea 6:6). Obedience was the law of innocency, but sacrifice supposes sin come into the world and is but a feeble attempt to take that away which obedience would have prevented. It is much easier to bring a bullock or lamb to be burnt upon the altar than to bring every high thought into obedience to God and the will subject to his will. Nothing is so provoking to God as disobedience, setting up our wills in competition with his. This is here called rebellion and stubbornness, and is said to be as bad as witchcraft and idolatry (v.23).

It is as bad to set up other gods as to live in disobedience to the true God... Those are unfit and unworthy to rule over men who are not willing that God should rule over them.

Testimony:

A great man of God, Kenneth Copeland, was in a meeting one day, and he said when they began to pass the offering bucket, all he had was the petrol in his car to take him back home. He said, as the bucket got near, he looked around and said, "God this opportunity cannot pass by me." He looked at his jacket and he had gold buttons on his jacket. He tore off the buttons and put them in the bucket as his offering. He had such an understanding of the principles that he could not afford to stand before God with an excuse for not giving back to God. This man of God today is an epitome of kingdom prosperity. But he started by recognizing that the altar of God is the place where destinies are altered. The altar of God is the furnace where your destiny is hammered into shape. The gift you bring to that altar is what represents you. That is where your destiny begins to be altered.

In Luke 21 the Bible says Jesus sat over the offering box watching what everybody was giving. What you give is important.

Testimony:

Sometime in the early part of the year 2000, I was serving in the great nation of Cameroon as a missionary. At that time by providence I was alone in the mission with my wife, running the church and the Bible school, performing also all the administrative functions that my assistant would otherwise have engaged in. I was patiently waiting for the headquarters to send me an assistant.

Contrary to my expectation, I received a letter that actually cut down my family allowances by $75 every month. At first it was demoralizing, and I thought I should contact the relevant officers and find out what was going on but then the Spirit of God ministered to me not to. One day I sat down and made a decision to increase my offering because I sincerely believed I deserved an increase not a decrease. From 15% of my income I increased my offering after tithes to 50% and I did this faithfully for six months before the heavens opened over my finances in a most dramatic way. By the sixth month someone walked up to me and gave me a one time offering that was three times my monthly allowance, at the same time two people paid independently for my laptop computer and all manner of favours began to flow to me. No one knew what I was doing except God, and my wife from whom I often had to squeeze some cash. God's faithfulness is so real.

Your tithe is like opening a bank account. It registers you and it establishes a relationship. What you give as offering is what determines what comes out of this relationship when the windows of heaven are opened. The tithe opens the window but what you give determines what comes out of that window from God to you.

THE LAW OF OBEDIENCE

In Ecclesiastes 11:1-3

"Cast thy bread upon the waters: for thou shalt find it after many days. Give a portion to seven, and also to eight; for thou knoweth not what evil shall be upon the earth. If the clouds be full of rain, they empty themselves upon the earth: and if the tree fall toward the south, or toward the north, in the place where the tree falleth, there it shall be."

There was a dimension of sacrificial giving which Abraham entered into in Genesis 22 that established his inheritance forever. The Bible says cast thy bread upon the water, remember that in 2 Corinthians 9:10, the Bible also says,

"Now he that ministereth seed to the sower both minister bread for your food, and multiply your seed sown, and increase the fruits of your righteousness."

In other words, everything that comes to you contains bread and seed. The bread is for you, but the seed is for you to sow to maintain the cycle of harvest and blessings. The realm of sacrifice is when you have sown your seed and also cast your bread. Why would you cast your bread? Because the Bible says in verse 3, "if the clouds be full of rain, they empty themselves upon the earth." In Genesis when God opened the windows of heaven, there was a flood. In the natural, when the cloud is full, no devil can stop the rain from falling. Somebody says I have been giving my offering when is my due season? When will my rain fall? Not until your cloud is full. So when you give, you are filling up your cloud. When you get to a desperate situation and things look tight, what do you do? You gather a sacrifice and fill that cloud quickly. When you gather your bread that is from God, that is given for you to enjoy and you sow it that is a sacrifice. When you have paid your tithe, you have given offering, but you need a breakthrough and you say, "God this is something I should enjoy of the labor of my hands but I sacrifice what I should enjoy to fill my cloud." Heaven will open.

In Ps 126:5-6 the Bible says,

> *"They that sow in tears shall reap in joy.*
> *He that goeth forth and weepeth, bearing precious seed, shall doubtless come again (doubtless i.e. without any doubt as long as God is God) with rejoicing, bringing his sheaves with him."*

When there is a project in the kingdom of God, it is also a time to make a sacrifice because it places a demand on you beyond your normal offering. Whenever God is doing something in the kingdom, maybe a building project, it is because God wants to build something in your life. Every project in the body of Christ reflects on the individuals who yield themselves to be involved in it. Your level of sacrificial participation is the level to which God builds you up. Some people when they hear that there is a project will shy away, saying, this Pastor has come again. No! It's for your own life.

Another way of returning to God is giving to the Prophets or His servants. In Matthew 10:41 Jesus said, *"he that receives a prophet in the name of a prophet shall have a prophets reward"* – Prophets are God's messengers sent to bless you. When you give to the one that is sent to you, you are indirectly giving to the one who sent him. And this always attracts a reward from God. You must take advantage of God's servants that are in your life. In 1 Corinthians 9:7-11, "Who goeth a warfare anytime at his own charges? (He is not there at his own expense somebody has sent him). Who planteth a vineyard, and eateth not of the fruit thereof. Or who feedeth a flock and eateth not of the milk of the flock? Say I these things as a man? Or sayeth not the Law the same also? For it is written in the Law of Moses, thou shalt not muzzle the mouth of the ox that treadeth out the corn. Doth God take care for oxen? Or saith, he it altogether for our sakes? For our sakes, no doubt, this is written: that he that ploweth should plow in hope; and that he that thresheth in hope should be partaker of His hope. If we have sown unto you spiritual things, is it a great

THE LAW OF OBEDIENCE

thing if we shall reap your carnal things?"

Galatians 6:6 says,

> *"Let him that is taught in the word communicate unto him that teacheth in all good things (In all good things that come into your life, you must share with him). Be not deceived; God is not mocked: whatsoever a man soweth, that shall he also reap."*

You need to provoke prophetic encounters. The widow of Zarepath had a prophetic encounter. There are some things you do that will provoke a blessing from the mouth of the instrument that God has put around you.

Even though the woman had lost everything and she was even ready to lose her life, she had enough sense, to recognize a man of God. When she gave to that man of God, she provoked a prophetic utterance that, "this cruse of oil and the barrel of meal shall not cease and what happened? Not only was she fed from it; she fed her entire household for about 3 years.

Look at the Shunamite woman in 2 Kings 4 she had a prophetic encounter with Elisha and God gave her a son via that prophetic encounter. The truth is that, when you care for God's servant, it will provoke God to care for you. Prophetic encounters don't die. When you provoke the heart of a man of God and a word of prophecy into your life, God says I will confirm the word of my servant, and perform the counsel of my messengers Isaiah 44:26. As long as that prophet was still around, the devil was helpless in corrupting the blessing that came via that prophetic encounter, he was defeated. The Shunamite woman received back her son alive and well.

In 2 Chronicles 20:20 the Bible says

> "...Believe in the Lord your God, so shall ye be established; believe his prophets so shall ye prosper."

In other words, your prosperity is tied to the instruments that God has put around you. If you despise them, you will go down. It is not a curse, but the truth.

In Luke 8:2-3, there were some women who ministered to Jesus of their substance not because He lacked or had a need, but they recognized that he was an instrument of God sent to bless them. Philippians 4:15 expresses Apostle Paul's understanding of this mystery, that your prosperity is tied to how you care for the instruments of God that He has put in your life. "Now ye Philippians know also, that in the beginning of the gospel, when I departed from Macedonia, no church communicated with me as concerning giving and receiving, but ye only (There is no giving without receiving. When you give, you will receive). For even in Thessalonica, ye sent once and again unto my necessity. Not because I desire a gift: but I desire fruit that may abound to your account."

When you properly receive God's servant who is genuinely serving God, and you take care of him, you are taking care of him for God. In other words, God will in turn take care of you. It is only for good to abound in your own account with God.

Giving to the less privileged is another scriptural way of obeying the law of giving. In this kingdom, Jesus said in Luke 16:11 that true prosperity is committed unto the trust of people that God can trust. If God cannot trust you, he will not entrust you with his true riches.

Psalm 41:1-3

"Blessed is he that considereth the poor: the Lord will deliver him in time of trouble. The Lord will preserve him, and keep him alive; and he shall be blessed upon the earth: and thou will not deliver him unto the will of his enemies. The Lord will strengthen him upon the bed of languishing. Thou will make all his bed in his sickness"
(that means he will never be sick). If God is now the nurse laying your bed, where will sickness hide?

Look at Proverbs 19:17
"He that hath pity upon the poor lendeth unto the Lord; and that which he had given will he pay him again."

Paul in 1 Timothy 6:17–18 charged the rich *"...that they be not high minded, nor trust in uncertain riches, but in the living God, who giveth us richly all things to enjoy; That they do good, that they be rich in good works ready to distribute, willing to communicate"* (give).

Until you flow out, nothing will flow in.

CHAPTER FIVE

THE LAW OF RECOGNITION

In Joshua 5:13-15 the Bible says,

> "And it came to pass, when Joshua was by Jericho, that he lifted up his eyes and looked, and behold there stood a man over against him with his sword drawn in his hand: and Joshua went unto him and said unto him, Art thou for us, or for our adversaries? And he said, Nay; but as captain of the host of the Lord, am I now come. And Joshua fell on his face and did worship, and said unto him, what saith my Lord unto his servant? And the captain of the Lord's host said unto Joshua, loose thy shoe from off thy foot; for the place whereon thou standest is holy. And Joshua did so."

Let me show you a comparative scripture to the law we are about to discuss in Acts 9:4-5

> "And he fell to the earth, and heard a voice saying unto him, Saul, Saul why persecutest thou me? And he said, Who art thou Lord? And the Lord said, I am Jesus whom thou persecutest: it is hard for thee to kick against the pricks."

You know many times I have heard some women praying for their husbands to get saved and they say, Lord I wish you give him an encounter like that of Saul. If you understand this encounter, you may pray differently. Do you know why? When

Jesus appeared to Saul, He did not appear to him to save him. He said, it is hard for thee to kick against the pricks. His sword was drawn. Thank God that Paul recognized who it was. He would have died on that spot. Jesus was there to stop him not to save him. Paul only had enough sense to get saved and was sent in the process.

The Bible says that the Captain of the Lord's host had his sword drawn. Thank God that Joshua recognized Him and he worked for him. Thank God that Paul also recognized him as Lord and submitted to His authority.

The truth is that, what you don't recognize, never works for you. What you don't acknowledge, will never work in your hand. The Holy Ghost is everywhere for instance but when you don't recognize Him, He will not work in your life. The power of God is everywhere, but when you don't recognize it, it doesn't work for you. There is a law of recognition. Many people fail because they despise certain things they should recognize. In Mark 5, we saw the woman with the issue of blood. And the Bible said she recognized Jesus when she had heard of Jesus, she recognized the anointing in his life. She must have said, I may not have the privilege of having an interview with Him, maybe there will be no chance for counseling, but Lord if I can just touch Him. She obeyed the law of recognition and what happened? She was made whole and Jesus said, "daughter thy faith has made thee well." There was a connection between what she recognized and what her faith could do.

Hebrews 11:6

"But without faith it is impossible to please him: for he that cometh to God must believe that he is, and that he is a rewarder of them that diligently seek him."

THE LAW OF RECOGNITION

Anyone who comes to Him must recognize whom He is; your recognition and pursuit of that which you can see of Him is the demonstration of your faith that pleases Him. Look at the story in 2Kings 4:1,

> "Now there cried a certain woman of the wives of the sons of the prophets unto Elisha saying, Thy servant my husband is dead; and thou knowest that thy servant did fear the Lord and the creditor is come to take unto him my two sons to be bondmen."

She said regarding her husband, "thou knowest." So Elisha was alive and he knew when that prophet was suffering in debt. But perhaps because he refused to recognize Elisha, he died indebted. That prophet was in the same city with Elisha and Elisha knew him and he knew Elisha yet he died because he refused to recognize what God had put in Elisha. Thank God his widow was wiser.

Consider also the man in Acts 3 who was healed of paralysis by Peter and John, do you think that was the first day he was there? The Bible says they put him there daily for almost forty years. Jesus must have passed by that same place and perhaps he was not healed because he did not recognize Jesus. The day when he chose to recognize Peter, who had Christ in him, he got his healing.

The widow in 2 Kings 4, after her husband the prophet died, had enough courage to recognize the prophet of God in their midst. And when she went to Elisha, he said, what should I do for you? This is similar to what Jesus asked a man called Batimaeus. One day, this blind man recognized the person passing by as Jesus and he cried out with all his heart, "son of David have mercy on me." His cry stopped Jesus. Recognition always stops Jesus, but then he still requested to know his desire. What do you want me to do for you? Batimaeus received his sight. This widow came to

Elisha because she understood the law of recognition. And what happened? Elisha said what hast thou in the house? And she said, "thine handmaid has nothing" she almost missed her miracle because she almost did not recognize what she had. There is something you have that is able to turn around your destiny. Thank God she remembered. She said wait a minute, there is something that I consider as nothing, it's just a bottle of oil, and Elisha said that is your miracle. There is money everywhere, there is wealth everywhere there is prosperity enough for everyone. God is not broke neither is His bank closed. What you recognize and how soon you recognize it determines the flow of prosperity into your life.

Somebody is carrying his problems all over the place. All he sees around him are problems. But the truth is that, inside every problem there is a breakthrough. You get paid in life for the level of problems you can solve. So if you run from problems, you run from rewards. If you can recognize the breakthrough, you will turn that problem into a testimony. It depends on what you give attention to; it depends on what you recognize.

There was this story of two men in Britain as told by Pastor Mathew Ashimolowo. They had inherited a little hill and they had done their best to farm that hill with no success. They were two brothers from the same mother and they lived to be very old. One died at the age of 75 years, the other died at the age of 77 years. These two men lived in abject poverty in the countryside doing their best to make a living from that land, planting and struggling year in, year out. None of them had enough money to marry a wife. When they died, it was discovered that the hill they were farming contained one of the largest deposits of gold in the British Isles. It became government property. They did not even have a son or a daughter. They were so poor they could not marry, but they were sitting on gold. Lord, open my eyes to see the treasures around me.

Whatever becomes familiar becomes common. You know, they have been sitting on it, they wake every morning, they see it, and so it became common. They never cared to recognize it: can there be something around you that you have not recognized? There are certain things God has deposited in your life, there is a gift that is so precious, that can bless the world, that can be a solution to entire destinies. But sometimes, you look at yourself because you are so familiar with yourself and you despise your gift. One of the first things you must learn to recognize is your gift. You need an education for foundation, but you need your gift for destiny. Your destiny is hidden in your talent, in your gift. You must recognize it. Do not throw it away because your mother does not like it or because somebody else says no to your exercising that gift.

I remember another story of one man, who went through medical school and became a doctor. A time came and the community gathered to honour him as the first person in that small village that had become a doctor. When the whole village gathered, they honoured him and gave him a plaque, the man burst into tears. His parents were embarrassed. They said, why is this man crying like this? He took the plaque and gave it to his father and said, "Now that I have spent my life fulfilling your vision, can you give me a chance now to pursue my own life?" Because his father had insisted he must be a doctor. He said to the audience, "This is not what I wanted to do with my life, I became a doctor for my father, and so let him have the plaque. Now that I have fulfilled your vision dad, can you allow me to fulfill mine?" God had called that man into music. He is a medical doctor who today owns one of the biggest recording studios in Lagos, Nigeria. When he sits behind the piano, you would be inspired by his dexterity. He has thrown away the stethoscope forever. That is where he was gifted. He composes music from his head like it was a joke. I used to be in the advertising industry and a number of times I've seen him work on a jingle. He will just sit and caress the piano and before you know it, he has brought out something that never existed before. An original score comes so easily to him.

You must recognize your gift. There is something unique about you. Don't throw it away. No one else can be like you. You are special. You are unique. Please parents; there is something in your son, and your daughter. Try to help them discover their gifts. Don't bend their necks to fulfill your own vision. Help them discover their gifts. The next thing we need to recognize is that the widow had something in her house she did not recognize. But thank God she recognized the voice of God from the servant of God.

In John 10:4-5, Jesus said my sheep hear my voice, the voice of a stranger they will not follow. Every time you come to the house of God, the voice of God is always speaking. You must recognize the voice of God. This has happened to me many times. God's servant will be preaching but within the message I will hear the voice of God's leading. If you hear only the voice of the Pastor, you have not come to church. Behind the voice of the Pastor there is the voice of God. During the opening prayer, there is God's voice, during praise and worship; there is the voice of God. I'm aghast when I see people irreverent in the presence of God, while the service is in progress, it is shocking to see some people discussing or just idling. All through the service when in God's presence, you can hear the voice of God. If only you can recognize those times as times when God can speak to you, you will become greatly blessed.

Something happened to me in 1994. There was something I believed God for. And it was the last day of December and that thing had not come and it was like God did not answer my prayer. But I was determined to praise God anyway. However some minutes after 11.00pm as we were crossing into the New Year, somebody came to me and said, "I have been looking for you," and he gave me a letter that contained the answer to what I had been praying for. Praise God.

Sometimes, it is at end of the service that God will speak to you. Some people will leave the church before the end of the service and miss God's package for them. You must be able to recognize the voice of God in the house of God. God can use anybody to speak to you. God has been trying to speak to some people for a long time, but they have been listening for God's voice in wrong places. It is in His presence, in His house that you will most likely hear His voice. I have experienced this personally. Sometimes I am in a service and God's servant is preaching, and he says open to chapter 10 and then he reads verse 4 – The Holy Ghost then says, look at verse 5. And as I look at verse 5, He says this is the answer to that problem you have been praying for. Sometimes it may not be in line with what God's servant is preaching, but it is in line with my particular problem at that time. If you are not sensitive in the spirit, you may miss it. But God is always speaking because Zion is a mountain of voices. May you recognize His voice when He speaks to you. You will no longer miss His voice, in the name of Jesus. You must recognize the voice of God in the house of God. Also you must recognize the voice of the enemy. Jesus said, a stranger's voice they would not follow. Any voice of doubt, discouragement or fear, is the voice of the enemy. You must know how to silence it. You must recognize the voice of the enemy before you can achieve your purpose. When Moses sent the spies into Canaan, some came and said that the land eats people. They said they were like grasshoppers. Satan deceived their hearts. No man is like a grasshopper to another man. That was gross exaggeration. So don't exaggerate your problems. There is no problem without a solution.

Somebody comes and says Pastor; my problem is very big, and I reply, "No problem is big with Jesus". He say's, "Pastor you don't understand, it has lingered for a long time". Can a problem be older than God is? Some people actually have more faith in their problems than in God. They recognize the problem more than they recognize God. So God says, "Since you have decided to marry that problem and you prefer that problem to me, I will leave you. When you are tired, seek for me. I am always interceding for you to be free from your problem, but you are always praying to strengthen your faith in the problem. When you don't recognize the answer to your problem or the solution you desire, you will pray the problem and reinforce it. As long as you don't recognize the solution you cannot experience it."

For instance a woman wants a child and she prays, "God can't you see, I can't have a child. Even the last pregnancy came down" and she starts to cry. That woman is only multiplying the problem because God says you shall have whatever you say. That prayer she prayed is a negative prayer. You should pray what you want; God already knows the problem. He only demands from you, "I hope you have enough sense to know the solution you desire". So you need first to recognize your solution. It will be easy for you to deny the voice of the enemy, when you already know the answer that you desire as every solution is in the word of God. The enemy will keep pointing you to the problem, while the Holy Ghost wants to point you to the solution. When you recognize the voice of the enemy, then you will be able to tell him, "Shut up Satan." It is written, "His thoughts towards me are good not evil." Some people say Pastor, "I just had a dream and in that dream I had a very terrible accident. That is why I have come to pray." Some people tell me, "Pastor, all my dreams always come true". Some people believe their dreams more than they believe the Word of God. God did not say dreams are part of the gifts of the Holy Spirit. It is not one of the gifts. God may decide to speak to us through dreams but be aware that sometimes when you sleep in the night, Satan can gain access to your mind through films and other audio-visual materials you have polluted your mind with earlier. If you are not careful, you will dream a nonsense dream that may discourage or depress you. The greatest standard to guide your life with is the Word of God. Even if an angel appears now and says something that cannot be proved by the Word of God, he is an agent of the devil. If an angel appears to you, the first things to ask for are scriptures to back whatever he is saying.

Testimony

Rev. Kenneth Hagin gave a testimony of when Jesus appeared to him and Jesus told him about the future. He said he asked for scriptures from Jesus. The Bible says, "In the mouth of two or more witnesses" a matter is confirmed. You can't tell me something that contradicts the Bible because the word of God is settled forever. Kenneth Hagin asked for at least two scriptures from the Lord to prove what He was telling him and he said Jesus told him, I will give you four and He gave him four scriptures that put his mind at rest.

So don't be deceived by the voice of the enemy. Maybe God has told you to march ahead and do a particular business. Then you confer with your friend who begins to sow seeds of discouragement in you, and he says, "One man that tried that business last year collapsed. In fact it's just because I like you. My closest friend in London tried it and within two weeks, everything scattered. That business is not good." And then fear enters your heart, you now decide to go back and pray again. You may not hear God the second time. Refuse to hear the voice of the enemy. Don't allow the devil to deceive you. If you don't recognize the voice of the enemy, you won't be able to stop him.

If God reveals something to you, He will also reveal to you

what to do. God will never put fear in your heart for He has not given you the spirit of fear but of power, of love, and of sound mind 2Timothy 1:7. Jesus said to His disciples, "… behold I give unto you power…" Luke 10:19 when He comes, He comes to empower us. Anything that comes to make you afraid is not from God. From now the enemy will not deceive you. You must recognize a deliverer when you see one. The truth is that the deliverers that God sends into our lives come in different ways. In 2 Kings 5:1, there was a man called Naaman. Two deliverers helped him to get healed. He was a great man, honourable, but he was a leper. He had a 'but' in his life, however God had appointed some deliverers to remove the 'but'. You must have enough wisdom and humility to recognize the deliverers God sends to you. The first deliverer was a little maid a servant to his wife. Should a mighty man listen to a slave or little maid?

But Naaman recognized the voice of a deliverer and decided to listen. In verse 11, when he got to Israel, pride almost robbed him of his miracle. Elisha refused to come out because he recognized who he was in God. Naaman was angry and must have said, "I thought He will come out and stand and shake and call on the name of his God and speak in tongues for one hour in order to solve my problem. I thought he will come and fast for three days and then tell me, he is going on a prayer project for one week. So that after he has prayed for one week, he can have enough power to declare that my problem is solved. He just sent his servant to me, to go and take a bath in the river, what effrontery. The man was angry and said they had better rivers in his country than the dirty River Jordan. He must have thought, "I have a swimming pool in my house, fully chlorinated and this man is telling me to go and do water baptism in River Jordan. What kind of nonsense are they preaching in his church?" If you are that prideful, that may be why the 'but' in your life is still remaining. Do you constantly rationalize the instructions of the servant of God he has sent to you? Thank God another deliverer came to Naaman, his servant came near him in verse 13 and said, "My father, if the prophet had requested for all your property, you would have given it to him in exchange for this leprosy that is the "but" in your life, how much rather, this simple instruction?

Testimony

In a Church in Nigeria, there was a woman who after four years of marriage had no child. She and her husband were believers and they were serving God. They had done everything they knew to do. Nothing seemed to be happening until her mother in-law came from the village and insisted she must follow her to a herbalist. She said, "If your God can't do it, let us go to the village. I have one man there, who will cook up some herbs for you." This young woman became so distressed. It was like an ultimatum and a challenge was given to her. One day, some children in the neighborhood came to play with her, one of them a young girl, about six years old came into the house and met her looking depressed; she said, "Auntie, why are you sad? Is it because you are not pregnant?" She said, "If I were you, I would act as if I am pregnant." The woman said to the child, "Shut up your mouth, what do you know about pregnancy, leave this place now." As soon as the child left, the Holy Spirit said to her, "Did you hear that child? What would you do if you were pregnant?" She went and bought maternity gowns and began to put them on to work. She began to buy baby things and do what a pregnant woman would normally do. And when her mother in law arrived, she told her that God has done it. Even in her office her colleagues saw her and said thank God, it is done.

In her testimony she said she saw her period for three months after that, she was menstruating yet wearing maternity gown. When she was sharing this testimony, the Pastor came up and asked her how she felt during those times, wearing a maternity gown while everybody believed she was pregnant when she

was not. She said, "At first, I was afraid, I even thought I was deceiving myself, but a time came when I knew I had crossed a point where God could not fail me now, I got to a point where I knew that for God to fail me now means God is dead because I will just die. I got to a point where I knew in my heart that God couldn't remove His hand because I had put my hand in His hand." This woman gave birth to a bouncing baby boy.
God spoke through that six-year-old girl. I pray that you will recognize and listen to the deliverers around you.

The deliverer is not always your uncle who is not born again that you keep going to because he has money. God may send a deliverer to you who may not be related or look like someone who can help. It may even be a book or a tape. There are some people since this year started, they have not bought or read one book, but ask how much food they have put in their stomach? They have never enriched their spirit with spiritually edifying materials. Your deliverer may be a book. There is a pastor who pastors a church called Resurrection Chapel. He was a condemned murderer, condemned to death because he killed someone. While on death row, awaiting execution by hanging, one of the wardens gave him a book. In the course of reading that Christian literature, he met with Christ. He discovered that he was not born to die like a chicken, and that he was born to win and he believed it. He gave his life to Christ believing that Christ already died for him. He reckoned, "It is true I deserve to die. I had killed somebody as a robber, but now I recognize that someone died for me. I don't have to die; I can now live my life for Him who died for me." Mysteriously, the time to execute him came and passed and nothing happened another year passed and then another. One day the Chief Judge of the State came to the prison and gave a presidential pardon to some prisoners and this man was included. The man is a successful Pastor today. He went and started a church because he said, "I was dead but now I am resurrected," and he called the church Resurrection Chapel.

His deliverance was inside that book he saw in somebody's hand. He could have died, but now he is alive. May God open your eyes to see your deliverers in Jesus name. I see God leading you in strange ways and sending deliverers in mysterious ways to guide you into the fulfillment of your destiny.

For Joseph, the deliverer was the butler. He got to his throne through one man who witnessed his gift. No matter the kind of prison you are in now, the deliverer that will be the instrument of your breakthrough will locate you.

Bishop David Oyedepo shared with us how he was imparted while watching the video of late Archbishop Benson Idahosa. He was watching the crusade the Archbishop held in Ibadan and as people were being healed he began to cry, he was so moved. He said suddenly he heard physical steps, somebody walked into the room, he could not see anybody because the room was dark, and the only illumination was from the television set. He said he heard those footsteps, it was so majestic and he was not afraid, but was full of awe. Then he felt a physical hand, rest on his back and something went down his spine. And since that day, he entered the realm of miracles. It was by contact with videotape. He shared another testimony with us, how in the United States of America he got to the hotel where he was to stay for a conference, and the bellhop who carried his luggage told him, Kenneth Copeland had stayed in the room he was booked into.

The Bishop said, he reasoned in his mind if Kenneth Copeland slept on this bed there is no sleep for me tonight. He said that night; he did not sleep because he believed in the grace of God on Kenneth Copeland for prosperity. The Bishop said he coveted that grace, so he asked God for it. He said he began to roll on that bed and he prayed for transference of grace.

When he eventually fell asleep, he had a dream where he saw a withered hand, and God told him to speak to it. He spoke to that withered hand and a fresh hand came out. And God said to him "from today, you enter the realm of creative miracles." He could have slept on that bed and nothing would have happened if he did not recognize the grace on another servant of God.

There was the testimony of one barren woman who was privileged to receive the Bishop when he came to the town where she was, to have a crusade. She prepared a room for God's servant, where he slept. After the meeting, he packed his bags and left. In her testimony, she said, she went on the bed and said, "God, even if you cannot answer my own prayer, I recognize this man of God, I recognize that you called him, at least you will answer him because he is your servant. She got pregnant and slapped the devil with a set of twins! Many people fail to recognize the things that God has made for their peace. But from now, you will see them. You must also recognize your weakness. Stay away from the point of your weakness. When you recognize it, it will not be a weakness anymore. A wise man of God said "Starve your weakness, don't give it food and don't give it opportunity. Starve it and promote your gift". If you are a man or woman and you don't recognize your weakness, you may be a fool because the strongest part of a chain is determined by the weakest link. So if you can't recognize your weakness and avoid it, you may soon have regrets in your life. But you will not see shame in Jesus mighty name.

Finally, you must recognize mentors. These are people that God has programmed in your life to take you from where you are to where you ought to be. You must recognize and observe them. The way God made this world is for us always to have mentors. Since you were born, you have always had a mentor. Your parents were your first mentors. By the time you got to school age your teachers became your mentors. Now when you are born again,

God will use His servants to mentor you. Observe your mentors. People come to church and just say, "I just want to be blessed," but the house of God is more than a place of blessing, it is a place of transformation through observation. In your marriage, do you observe and study to blend with your spouse? Maybe your parents did not mentor you well, but in church God can transform you. Maybe your teachers mentored you wrongly, but in church God can change you. It is more than just coming to be blessed, and receiving the prophetic word from your Pastor.

No! You observe and you learn. For instance, I tell the leaders in church, I will not wear a T-shirt to Church, because I respect the altar of God. If I am going to meet the president of my country today, I will not dress carelessly. So why should I come and climb God's altar dressed anyhow. If bankers respect their place of work by going there properly dressed, I must also respect the God to whom I have come. I won't come in bathroom slippers like somebody going to the market. If I have only one shirt and pair of trousers, I will make sure I clean and iron them before I come into His presence. God has given mentors to help to mould us. We must learn from them. God always surrounds us with people that we can learn from. Those who are your friends may tell you, you are okay. But when you have a mentor, he will keep putting pressure on you to get better. When you have a mentor, you are like a football and your mentor is the player.

What is the aim of a football?
To score; it is when a ball enters the net that everybody rejoice and shout "It's a goal". The aim of your mentor is for you to score your goal in life so that people can clap for you. But ask the ball how it feels when they kick it. Sometimes your mentor appears to be kicking you. Sometimes he seems to dribble you; sometimes he is just pushing you here and there. Sometimes it's very difficult for you to do what he demands. The objective is for you to score. And when you score in your life, you will say,

"Thank God for that man or woman".

I read of one great man of God in Russia, who has one of the biggest TV ministries in Russia today, an American. He said he was serving as Youth Pastor under an anointed man of God and he admired that man so much and wanted to do everything to please that man. They usually had weekly meetings where they report the activities of their department; he could hardly wait for these weekly briefings. One day, he was so full of pride, as soon as it was his turn; he got up and began to say the things that he thought he had achieved but his mentor stopped him and said, "That's Ok". He was expecting the man to tell everybody to clap for him. The mentor removed his shoes in the presence of everybody and said, "I scraped my shoes this morning can you kindly take it out and clean it for me." He said he felt so humiliated that he wanted to resign. But today, he is eternally grateful for how that man carefully handled him and killed the pride that was in his heart. He said because he was young in ministry and was so full of pride, he thought he was better than everybody else. He was always looking for somebody to praise him. And when they came for departmental meetings his mentor would say, "Please go and wash my car." He said he would be angry, that this man did not recognize his anointing. In fact, he said that there was a time when because of his immaturity, he began to see his mentor's weaknesses. But the man of God carefully handed him and shook every bit of pride out of him. Today when he writes his autobiography, he will include the name of that servant of God and say, I would have lost my destiny if not for this man.

But I tell you when that man was kicking him and dribbling him, he felt like an angry ball would feel on a football field. But now, his life has scored. He is a worldwide name now. Don't become too familiar to spiritual mentors who can help you because you may loose your blessings. Sometimes your mentor says something and you can't understand it, but because he sees the goal better than you can, it is wise to carefully consider what is advised and obey. When you despise instruction, you may not be able to escape destruction. It is important to always pray for the Lord to teach us the law of recognition so that it will not fail in our lives. Lord, help me to recognize opportunities, mentors, and deliverers. Lord, help me put value on everyone you put around me, to recognize my gifts, the voice of God in the house of God, and the voice of the enemy. Lord everything shall go well with me from now as I put this law of recognition into practice. No opportunity will slip out of my life anymore.

CHAPTER SIX

THE LAW OF IDENTIFICATION

It is not enough to obey God in your tithes, in your offerings, in your prophet offerings, in your giving to the poor; you must fully identify with God.

What do I mean by identification. In Joshua 3:1-5 the Bible said,

> *"Joshua rose early in the morning; and they removed from Shittim, and came to the Jordan, he and all the children of Israel and lodged there before they passed over. And it came to pass after three days, that the officers went through the host: and they commanded the people, saying when ye see the ark of the covenant of the Lord your God, and the priests, the Levites bearing it, ye shall remove from your place and go after it. Yet there shall be a space between you and it, about two thousand cubits by measure (talking about respect): come not near unto it, that ye may know the way by which ye must go, for ye have not passed this way heretofore. Joshua said unto the people, sanctify yourselves..."*

Now the truth is, if you are born again, you have become a priest unto God. That is what the Bible tells us in Revelations 5:10.

See what God admonishes concerning those who bear the Ark of God – "Depart ye, depart, go out from there, touch no unclean thing, go out of the midst of her, be ye clean, that bear the vessels of the Lord". Isaiah 52:11

Abraham was so fully identified with God, that when Melchisedek saw him, he identified him with God in Genesis 14:18. Melchisedek was a type of Jesus who recognized Abraham's identification with God because like Jesus, he knew all things that was in all men. When Melchisedek brought forth bread and wine to share communion with Abraham, it was similar to what Jesus did in Mathew 26 with His disciples. There is an eternal mystery in the communion; it is the sharing of life, the meeting point of the mortal and the divine. The Bible says Melchisedek was the priest of the Most High God who blessed and addressed Abraham as; "… Abraham of the Most High God." Abraham was so identified with God that his name could not be called without the mention of God. Abraham also recognized who he was identified with.

This was demonstrated when Abraham met the king of Sodom. "And the king of Sodom said unto Abram, Give me the persons, and take the goods to thyself. (Remember that God later destroyed Sodom because it was a place of wickedness and evil). And Abram said to the king of Sodom, I have lifted up my hand unto the Lord, (to swear and to identify with) the Most High God, possessor of heaven and earth. That I will not take from a thread, even to a shoe latchet, and that I will not take any thing that is thine, lest thou shouldest say, I have made Abram rich" Genesis 14:21-23.

Our God that we identify with is the possessor of Heaven and Earth and our level of identification with God will determine the level of our business explosion. In Job 22:21 the bible says, "acquaint now thyself with Him and be at peace. And then good will come to you." Your level of identification with God will determine how blessed you will be on this earth. Abraham refused the booty from Sodom because the priest of the most high God just told him who he was. He was not in doubt as to the ability of the possessor of heaven and earth to provide for him.

Many people are playing games in church because they have lost their identification with God. No matter the tithe you pay, no matter the offering you give, if your life is not right, God cannot accept it. In Genesis 4:10, God first accepted the person of Abel before He accepted his offering. Your person must first be accepted, before whatever you give can be accepted, because whatever you give represents you. Abraham was so identified with God that when God wanted to do something on the earth in the terrain of Abraham, He said He couldn't do this thing without telling His friend. It was the force of identification. Identification was the greatest secret of Abraham. If you study the book of Genesis, you discover that wherever Abraham got to, the first thing he did was to build an altar, a place of communion because he delighted in communing with God. He wouldn't dare to do anything to disappoint his God.

Look at John 15 and tell me why you wouldn't wish for the friendship of God. The Bible called Abraham the friend of God. Who would not desire a relationship like that? It is not by lobbying but by working it out. John 15:14, "you are my friends if ye do whatever I command you". You can only become a friend of God when you do what He commands. That is the truth, look at John 8:29 and hear what Jesus Christ said, *"And he that sent me is with me. The Father hath not left me alone; for I do always the things that please him."*

He said God is not with me because I had a virgin birth, neither is God with me because He sent the Holy Ghost to me. You can have the Holy Ghost and still not obey God. Not everybody obeys God because God will never go against your will. He will try to guide you, but He will not force you, ever! Mary our Lord's mother said, "Whatever He tells you to do, do it." If you like, put your Bible under your pillow, it can't change you, maybe you carry yours like a talisman. Where God needs to change us is in our hearts. And that is what Jesus was saying here in verse 29. He that sent me is with me (not because my birth was announced or a virgin gave birth to me) but because after I got here, I began to do all the things that please Him. If you can be fully identified with God then God will fully identify with you. If you say you are a born again Christian, yet in your business you are doing dishonest things and you think it does not matter, you keep saying that is how we do it, the Pastor does not understand, he does not know about this business. This is the only way we do it. God won't be in that business. So you think God does not know about your business or about your country. If you stand with God, everything will change to stand with you. Abraham did not receive what the king of Sodom wanted to give him. But the Bible said God blessed him in all things. God will bless you in all things too; but you must be fully identified with Him.

God is a loving Father, but if you don't relate to Him in that truth you may not experience his goodness, too many people are deceitful, full of face, but no faithfulness. They can cry and worship especially when a powerful worship singer is leading worship, however when it comes to acting out in real life their love for God they make excuses. They say God you should understand; then God becomes their brother. They are ready for God to have part of their life but not all of it. This one is business, no church here now, God you can stay in the sitting room but don't come inside this bedroom, because this is business, don't concern yourself with this one. Rest assured that He would make sure that in every other thing, He doesn't show his concern. There are some people now in their business, going about it in the wrong way and they know it. Many in their business have serious problems because they didn't put God in the beginning, and when the ship is in the middle of the sea, without God, they now want God! You never identified with Him in the beginning. If the foundation is destroyed what can the righteous do? Proper identification in the beginning will keep God identifying with you in the middle and at the end. Do you fear God? Do you reverence Him? Do you respect Him? If you don't respect Him, if you don't fear Him, there is no way you can identify with Him because God says you must reverence Him. That is the truth because He is our creator. You can only become his friend when you respect Him and obey His commands. To identify with God, you must sanctify yourself because He is a Holy God, you can't walk disorderly and hope to be identified with Him. Those who bear the Ark must not touch unclean things. I see God sanctify your business today.

In 2 Timothy 2:19, the Bible says,

"Nevertheless the foundation of God standeth sure, having this seal. The Lord knoweth them that are His. Let everyone that nameth the name of Christ depart from iniquity."

It is not only expedient for you to want to appropriate everything that belongs to you. It is not enough to be prepared; many have prepared yet have failed, why? They could not walk with God. It is not just enough to obey the law of giving. In Job 22:23 the bible says "...thou shalt put iniquity very far from thy tabernacle." Why? He cannot be revealed in His mercy to you until you are ready to give away that iniquity. In their business many people still have funny friends and alliances with whom they do things the wrong way. If the government of your nation has laws governing business, why do you think God does not have a law concerning business? You can break the law of your country, maybe you won't be caught, but when you break the law of God, there are always consequences; it may not be now but it is always there.

The foundation of God stands sure. Everyone that is named by the name of Christ must depart from iniquity. I see God bring your life into limelight. You are the one that will determine what you want to be. He said in a great house, there are not only vessels of gold and of silver, but also of wood and of earth. Some unto honour some to dishonor. From these you make your choice, so God won't come and drag you out of the place where you are, the wrong bed where you are sleeping, the wrong business that you are doing. You are the one to purge yourself. You shall be a vessel unto honour, sanctified and fit for the master's use and then prepared unto every good work in Jesus name.

Three Consequences Of Purity

1. Divine Insight

In Mark 4:11, Jesus was speaking to His disciples. He said, *"Unto you it is given to know the mystery of the kingdom of God; but unto those who are without (those who are outside the kingdom) all these things are done in parables."* Being out of God's righteousness blocks our understanding and hinders vision. God wants to turn on his lights in you but you have a choice to receive or reject that offer John 3:16-21.

Who are those without that Jesus is referring to here that the kingdom of God will remain a mystery to? They belong to the company that will never understand the things of God as long as they refuse to let go of iniquity and keep rejecting God's light. Divine truth will remain a parable. Who are those outside? Revelation 22:14-15 tells us in verse 14, those who are inside and in verse 15 those who are outside. "Blessed are they that do his commandments, that they may have right to the tree of life, and may enter in through the gates of the city. For without are dogs and sorcerers and whoremongers, and murderers and idolaters and whosoever loveth and maketh a lie".

Who are dogs? Look at 2 Peter 2:22. "But it happened unto them according to the true proverb, the dog is turned to his own vomit again and the sow that was washed, to her wallowing in the mire".

The person who keeps going back to sin is referred to as a dog. Those who keep repenting and going back, they are the ones God says are dogs and when the day of reckoning comes He will keep them outside. A double-minded man can never receive anything from the Lord (James 1:8). They will never receive revelation. It will always remain a mystery and their life will always remain in misery.

Your life will not be in misery in Jesus mighty name. It takes purity to have insight. The Bible says in 2 Peter 1:20-21 as regards the holy men of God who received the word, "Knowing this first, that no prophecy of the scripture is of any private interpretation, for the prophecy came not in old time by the will of man, but holy men of God spake as they were moved by the Holy Ghost."

They were first holy before the Holy Spirit could move on them to understand the mystery, to understand the truth. In other words, ungodliness hinders revelation, veils vision, and blocks direction.

2. *The Anointing*

The anointing will only work in your life to the degree to which you are pure.

In Psalm 45:6 the Bible says,

> *"Thy throne O God is forever and ever: the sceptre of Thy kingdom is the right sceptre. Thou lovest righteousness, and hatest wickedness: therefore God, thy God had anointed thee with the oil of gladness above thy fellows."*

God will not anoint you until you hate wickedness and you love righteousness. You must love to do things right. What is not right is wrong. There is no middle way. Jesus said because you are neither hot nor cold, I will spit you out of my mouth. There is no gray area when it comes to sin. You are either black or white. You can't say you are just in between; I am in the grey region where white and black meets, No! You are either white or black. Luke 5:36-38 says the degree to which you keep yourself pure, is the degree to which the anointing of God can rest upon your life – "No man putteth a piece of a new garment upon an old; if otherwise, then both the new maketh a rent, and the piece that was taken out of the new agreeth not with the old. And no man putteth new wine into old bottles; else the new wine will burst the bottles and be spilled, and the bottles shall perish. But new wine must be put into a new bottles; and both are preserved."

The anointing is what is called the new wine. The old thing in your nature you are keeping is the reason why the anointing has not come to rest. Until you let go of certain things, you cannot let in the power of God. Until you decide to be new, you can't have the new power of God. That thing you are holding on to is what is keeping you from achieving your destiny. You say, "Pastor, it is just difficult." That is why your life is difficult. Until you let go you cannot enter into God's rest. "It is not by power; it is not by might, but by My Spirit." Zechariah 4:6 He promised to send you a helper. Ok the helper has come and he says I want to help you, but you say, "Wait first helper, I am holding onto something here, this is what will help me." As long as it is difficult to leave that thing, your life will remain difficult. Let go that thing and you will see the anointing and the help of God.

Purity allows the anointing of God to rest upon your life.

3. *Divine Power*

Jesus said in John 8:29, "My Father hath not left me alone; because I do always those things that please Him". In Acts 10:38, "How God anointed Jesus of Nazareth with the Holy Ghost and with power, who went about doing good, healing all that were oppressed of the devil; for God was with Him."

When God is with you, every mountain will bow before you. He is a Holy God. To guarantee His presence with you, you must keep yourself pure. A man of God Benny Hinn said, "I thank God, by His grace, I have managed to keep myself pure, because I understand that the power of God flows through me." And if you are the vessel through whom that power will flow, you can either block it or reduce it by what kind of vessel you are."

You are destined as a vessel of honor in the hand of God. Do you know that? If you are born again, you are already called unto a ministry, the ministry of reconciliation. He said you shall be witnesses unto Me. How much of a witness are you? Can people look at your life and say; "Ok we will follow you to church." There are some people who are such terrible examples that others refuse to come to Christ. In other words, God destined you to come into the way and show to other people the way. But when you have come into the way, do you block other people from the way because of the way you live your life? Do people say of you, "If that is a Christian, I don't want to be one".

You are in business and you have an unbeliever partner but because you don't want to give a bribe you allow your partner to do so. You even encourage him to just do whatever he needs to do. After all you are the one giving the bribe. How do you think that man will get saved? He can't get saved. Because when you are talking about Christ, he says in his mind, "My friend, we are in this thing together; what church matters are you telling me now, please leave me alone." Why? Because you are in the shady business thing together even though you try to pacify your own conscience that after all you were not the one giving the bribe. But you are sending someone else to do it. You are a thief too. Both the person that went to steal and the man who sent him to steal; what are they together? Thieves. God is not mocked.

Look at Psalm 15:1-5,

"Lord who shall abide in thy tabernacle, who shall dwell in thy Holy hill? He that walketh uprightly and worketh righteousness and speaketh the truth in his heart. He that backbiteth not with his tongue nor doeth evil to his neighbor, nor taketh up a reproach against his neighbor. In whose eyes a vile person is despised, but he honoureth them who fear the Lord. He that sweareth to his own hurt and changeth not. He that putteth not out his money to interest, nor taketh reward against the innocent. He that doeth those things, shall never be moved."

I want to show you something our Lord Jesus said in John 17:19 and I want you to be able to make a decision for God today, to walk with God, to sanctify yourself. To walk with God is to not have a consciousness of sin in your heart, to believe in the power of the blood and to walk in a pure conscience. In verse 19 Jesus said, *"And for their sakes I sanctify myself, that they also might be sanctified through the truth".*

Some of you, your family members have refused to be born again because of you. If you sanctify yourself for their sake, they will soon be sanctified too. Some of you, your staff in the office, are not born again because of you. If you will live a sanctified life, they will soon join you. Speak to God and say, "Lord, I want to be a witness for you. That is the main purpose why you saved me. I want my life to be a living proof of the life, death and resurrection of the Lord Jesus Christ. I don't just want to carry the label of Christianity; I want people to see Christ in me. Not just by attending church, or carrying a Bible, but by how I live. Let me live for you Lord, let my life be identified with you. Let the people in my neighborhood be able to say, that woman or man is of God. Lord, make me a faithful witness for you in all I do with the business of my life." Always remember that the people who are observing you are more than the people you can see.

Prophetic Utterrance

- May that grace to fully identify with God, to be buried and resurrected with Him, is deposited in your life today
- Every old nature, I see them drop out of your life
- Everything that has been a hindrance in your going forward in life, I see it flushed out of your life.
- I see the blood of Jesus cleanse you this day and make you a true witness for God. In the name of Jesus Christ … (Amen)

www.ingramcontent.com/pod-product-compliance
Lightning Source LLC
Chambersburg PA
CBHW061456040426
42450CB00007B/1376